LED ZEPPELIN

A Visual Documentary by Paul Kendall

Omnibus Press

London/New York/Sydney/Cologne

© Copyright 1982 Omnibus Press
(a division of Book Sales Limited)

ISBN 0.7119.0094.9
UK Order No: OP 41896

Exclusive Distributors:
Book Sales Limited
8/9 Frith Street. London WIV 5TZ England.
Omnibus Press
120 Rothschild Avenue.
Rosebery. NSW 2018.
Australia

To The Music Trade Only:
Music Sales Limited
8/9 Frith Street, London WIV 5TZ England.

Art directed by Mike Bell.
Designed by Laurence Bradbury.
Assisted by Fiona Barlow.
Picture research by Valerie Boyd.
Front cover photographs by David Redfern,
London Features International, Pictorial Press.
Back cover photographs by Camera Press, London
Features International, Pictorial Press, David
Redfern.
Typeset by Futurafoto, London.
Printed in Japan by Dai Nippon Printing Co. Ltd.
Tokyo.

Special thanks to Howard Mylett, one of the world's
greatest authorities on Led Zeppelin, for all his
help in the preparation of this book.

Thanks to Angie Errigo for all her help. Every effort
has been made to trace the copyright holders of the
photographs in this book but one or two were
unreachable. We would be grateful if the
photographers concerned would contact us.

Picture Credits Atlantic Records 8TR, 15, 18/19L.
Camera Press 5BL, 8BL, 8BR, 10TL, 27TL, 38TC,
39BR, 42BL, 42C, 66/67, 68-69. Richard Creamer
44BR. Andre Csillag 45TR, 45CR, 45B, 52TR,
56BL, 86B, 94/95C. Kevin Cummins 87B. C.M.C.
Dunn 25BR, 41TL. Robert Ellis 20BL. Brad
Elterman 58/59. Epic 73TR. Brian Evans 72.
Simon Fowler L.F.I. 2/3, 78, 87T. Jill Furmanovsky
53, 83. Bob Gruen 9TL. Gijsbert Hanekroot 29BL,
30TL, 30BC, 32TL. Alan Johnson 28R. Lancashire
Evening Post 37BL, 37TR. L.F.I. 4BR, 5MR, 7BL,
9BL, 9BR, 10BL, 12, 31, 41BR, 44C, 46BL, 46MR,
47BR, 50BL, 51 (and insets), 54T, 55BR, 62B,
63TL, 73ML, 80TL, 81, 84/85, 90/91C,
93T&B. Janet Macoska 63TR. Ken Macpherson
74BL. Melody Maker 16/17, 17BR, 21TL, 22TL,
22BC, 29TR, 30BR. Barry Plummer 4BL, 4ML,
8TL, 10ML, 24/25C, 25TR, 27TR, 33TL, 44ML,
44TC, 44BC, 62BL, 73BL, 82TC, 82MC, 82CL.
Pictorial Press 7BR, 11B, 34BR, 47TR, 48BR,
50ML, 50TR, 62TR. Neal Preston L.F.I. T, 76/77,
86T. Michael Putland L.F.I. 30BL, 46BR. David
Redfern 15 inset, 39, 54B. Rex Features 5BR,
10MR, 10BR, 11TL. Kate Simon 56T. Pennie Smith
52TL, 57TL. Swansong 60/61, 70/71. Syndication
International 5TR, 13TR, 26BL, 64BL. Mathew
Taylor 10TR, 80ML. Chris Walter 63BL.

Jimmy Page

Born James Patrick Page on January 9th, 1944, at Heston, Middlesex. The only son of an industrial personnel officer and a doctor's secretary.

After living for some time on an uncle's farm in Northamptonshire, the family moved to Miles Road in Epsom, Surrey, when Jimmy was about eight. At school he sang in the choir, became school hurdles champion and was a keen artist. But when his parents gave him a Spanish guitar in 1957, that became his over-riding passion.

Apart from a few basic lessons with a teacher in nearby Kingston-on-Thames, he was self-taught. He recalls having his guitar confiscated on numerous occasions when he took it to school to practise between, and even during, classes.

He didn't really turn on to rock 'n' roll, however, till he heard 'Baby, Let's Play House' from the album 'A Date With Elvis', which came out around mid 1959.

Shortly after that he left school and, having tried unsuccessfully to get a job as a laboratory assistant, accepted an invitation to join Neil Christian and The Crusaders, who had spotted him playing in a local dance hall.

These gentlemen were anticipating the British Blues Boom by several years, playing Chuck Berry and Bo Diddley numbers and other stuff picked up from imported records. The great music-loving public weren't quite ready for it, but among other musicians the 15-year-old Jimmy Page soon began to build a considerable reputation.

Jeff Beck remembers: "Page was raving around with this big Gretsch Country Gentleman guitar, and it looked huge on him because he was such a shrimp. He was even smaller than he is now. So all you saw was this huge guitar being wielded around by a man who was as thin as a pipe cleaner. But I must say I was most impressed by his ability. He used to play fiery sort of fast stuff. The trouble was that no-one was listening to it."

Another problem was that the endless routine of bashing round the country in a van took its toll on Page's health. A bout of glandular fever was the final straw and his two-year stint with the group came to an end.

At this point he went back to his other great love, painting, attending art college for 18 months between mid 1961 and early 1963. Music was never ignored, though. Jam sessions at the Page household

with various friends, including Jeff Beck, were commonplace. And as R&B fever took a grip on the London music scene, he became a frequent visitor to clubs like Richmond's Crawdaddy, the Eel Pie Island in Twickenham, and the Marquee. At the latter he became involved with Cyril Davies' Rhythm & Blues All Stars, one of several groups of the era that were great breeding grounds for future stars. Long John Baldry and Nicky Hopkins were just two of the musicians who went on to greater things after working with Davies.

Page played with them only occasionally, but that was enough to get him noticed by producer Mike Leander, who invited him to play on a recording session in late 1962.

The outcome of the session was 'Diamonds' by Jet Harris and Tony Meehan. It took them to No. 1, and

launched our young hero on a new career. The only session guitarist of note at the time was Big Jim Sullivan, and the arrival of a new talent was welcomed like rain in the desert.

Pausing only to take a crash course in reading and writing music, Jimmy promptly became a super-sessioneer, playing on literally hundreds of recordings during the next three and a half years.

These varied from rock and pop groups, to big bands like Burt Bacharach and Johnny Dankworth, to sessions for jingles and soundtracks. And, not surprisingly, they also varied from the epic to the totally naff. The former included stuff for The Who, The Kinks and Them. The latter are too numerous to mention.

In between all this he found time to do a spot of songwriting with Jackie de Shannon, to form his own publishing company, and to record his own single for Fontana in 1965. This was a little thing called 'She Just Satisfies', backed by 'Keep Moving'. Page played all the instruments on it, apart from the drums. He even sang. In retrospect he probably wishes he hadn't bothered.

Also during 1965 came an invitation to be A&R man for ex-

Stones manager Andrew Oldham's new label, Immediate. Part of this job was to be producing a special British blues series, and that included Eric Clapton, who had become a close friend.

The tracks Page recorded with Clapton – 'Telephone Blues', 'I'm Your Witch Doctor', 'Sittin' On Top Of The World' and 'Double Crossin' Time' – have cropped up in various places since, and are pretty good.

But, unfortunately, some other tracks recorded informally at the

The Yardbirds

The Yardbirds had been a prominent part of the British R&B scene ever since their formation in late 1963. They had taken over The Rolling Stones residency at the Crawdaddy in Richmond when The Stones moved on to greater things, and their versions of American R&B classics, featuring guitarist Eric 'Slowhand' Clapton, earned them a fanatical following in and around London.

Before long, however, they moved on to more commercial pastures, drawing on material from publisher's songwriter Graham Gouldman, who would later make his name with 10cc. Clapton resigned in protest at this, and in February 1965 Jimmy Page, who had been friendly with the group for some time, was offered the guitarist's job.

"If I hadn't known Eric, or hadn't liked him, I might have joined. As it was, I didn't want any part of it. I liked Eric quite a bit and I didn't want him to think I'd done something behind his back," said Page, explaining his rejection of the offer.

Instead, he recommended Jeff Beck and for the next year The Yardbirds enjoyed a string of hits on both sides of the Atlantic. Then,

Page home were also put out on an Immediate anthology, despite opposition from Jimmy, and the ensuing confusion and dispute put an end to the friendship.

By 1966, Jimmy had just about had enough of the session routine. Opportunities to do something interesting in that field were getting increasingly rare, and when his mates The The Yardbirds needed helping out, when their bass player left in the summer of that year, he was perfectly willing to step in.

in the summer of 1966, the group had reason to call on the guitarist's services once again.

"They were playing in front of all these penguin-suited undergraduates and I think Samwell-Smith (The Yardbirds bass guitarist), whose family were a bit well-to-do, was embarrassed by the band's behaviour. Apparently Keith Relf had gotten really drunk and was falling into the drum kit, making farting noises into the mike – being generally anarchistic. I thought he'd done really well, actually, and the band played really well that night. When he came off-stage, though, Paul Samwell-Smith said 'I'm leaving the band'. Things used to be so final then.

Jeff had brought me to the gig in his car and on the way back I told him I'd sit in until they got things sorted out . . . It was decided we'd definitely have a go at it. I'd take on the bass though I'd never played it before, but only until Dreja (the rhythm guitarist) could learn it – he'd never played it before either. We figured it would be easier for me to pick up quickly, then switch over to a dual guitar thing when Chris (Dreja) had had time to become sufficiently familiar with the bass."

Page played his first date with The Yardbirds at the Marquee, after only about two hours rehearsal, and what had begun as a short-term helping hand for some friends ended up as a two year stint until the group's final demise.

In many ways, Page had joined at a bad time. The Yardbirds were having management problems, having lost their original guiding light, Giorgio Gomelsky, and were going through a few internal ructions, caused mainly by the erratic behaviour of Jeff Beck.

Nevertheless, although their days of big hit singles were over, they were still a strong live attraction, especially in the States, where

and I wasn't exactly ready to roar off on lead guitar. But it went all right and after that we stayed that way. When Jeff recovered it was two lead guitars from then on."

This potentially dynamic combination was unfortunately short-lived, and left only the 'Happenings Ten Years Time Ago'/'Psycho Daisies' single as a hint of how amazing it could have been. By the end of 1966, the rest of the group had decided they couldn't work with Beck any more, and he was elbowed.

At about the same time, The Yardbirds also parted company with manager Simon Napier-Bell. Despite having toured almost constantly for several months, they were regular visitors. Page's first major tour with them was a package tour of the UK with The Rolling Stones, Ike & Tina Turner and Peter Jay & The Jay Walkers, which opened at the Albert Hall on September 23rd, 1966. From there they went to the States, and Page found himself thrust unexpectedly into the limelight.

"The switch (from bass to lead) was necessitated earlier than planned. We were playing a gig at the Carousel Club in San Francisco, and because Jeff couldn't make it I took over lead that night and Chris Dreja played bass. It was really nerve-wracking, because this was at the height of The Yardbirds' concert reputation

appearing in Antonioni's film 'Blow Up', and doing various jingles for TV commercials, the individual members of the group had ended up with almost nothing to show for it. The man brought in to sort things out was Peter Grant.

"Peter was working for Mickie Most and was offered the management when Most was offered the recording, of which the first session on our behalf was 'Little Games' and the first on Beck's behalf was 'Love Is Blue'. I'd known Peter from way back in the days of

Immediate, because our offices were next door to Mickie Most's, and Peter was working for him. The first thing we did with him was a tour of Australia and we found that suddenly there was some money being made after all."

The new management situation seemed to work out well, but the recording arrangement with Mickie Most certainly did not. None of the singles made with him were successful, commercially or artistically, and the one album they managed to assemble, 'Little Games', was little short of a mess.

"It was just so bloody rushed", Page recalls. "Everything was done in one take because Mickie Most was basically interested in singles and didn't believe it was worth the time to do the tracks right on the album."

In fact, 'Little Games' was released only in America, where The Yardbirds were now spending more and more of their time. They also toured Australia and the Far East in early 1967, and Japan shortly before the group finally

called it a day after a gig at Luton Technical College in July 1968.

"Over the months before the split, Relf and McCarty (Keith Relf, the singer, and Jim McCarty, the drummer) had been talking about starting up a new scene. To counteract the sort of stuff I was listening to, they were into very light things like Simon & Garfunkel, The Turtles and people like that, and they wrote some songs in that vein, which they wanted to go off and record.

I was in favour of us keeping the group together and tried to persuade them to stay and record their songs as The Yardbirds, because I knew we had the potential to pull it off – but they just wouldn't have any of it."

Relf and McCarty formed Renaissance and Chris Dreja, who originally intended staying with Jimmy Page to form a New Yardbirds, decided instead to try a new career in photography. One of his first commissions would be the sleeve shots for the first Led Zeppelin album.

John Paul Jones

Born John Baldwin on January 3rd, 1946, at Sidcup, Kent. With a father who was pianist and arranger for big bands like the Ambrose Orchestra, and a mother who was a singer and dancer, it is hard to imagine how John Paul Jones could have avoided getting involved with show business.

As a youngster, he learnt the basics of piano playing at the family's home in Eltham. Then he started taking organ lessons, and was soon playing at his local church.

While attending Christ College boarding school in Blackheath, he turned to the bass. "I couldn't even play a six-string acoustic guitar when I started", he says. "I was just fascinated by bass work generally. I used to turn up the bass on my records and listen to the runs, and in time I just picked it up."

At school he formed a group which played American Air Force bases, and in the holidays he joined his father in a duo that played

various social functions, and even did a residency on the Isle of Wight.

When he left school, he continued this sort of work for a few months, until the day he attended an audition for ex-Shadows Jet Harris and Tony Meehan in early 1963.

Tony Meehan remembers: "We had a single called 'Diamonds' at Number 1 at the time and we were putting together a band. John Paul heard about it and showed up. He was just out of school, very young and a bit nervous. Despite the nerves he was a good musician and he knew his shit. He was cocky too in a certain way, and I liked that. So we hired him.

He toured with us for a year or 18 months until the band broke up. I was doing some freelance produc-

tion work for Decca Records at the time, and he played on a lot of sessions. I liked to use the guys from the band – they knew their shit and it supplemented their incomes. They were making about £40 per week in the band, which was good bread in those days. Add to that the session income and TV fees . . . all told, it was a good gig for them."

Jones continued playing sessions when the Harris/Meehan band split up, and between 1964 and 1968 recorded for just about everyone from Lulu to The Rolling Stones. In April 1964 he released his own single on Pye, comprising two instrumentals called 'A Foggy Day In Vietnam' and 'Baja', and before long he had graduated from ordinary sessionman to musical director.

"I discovered that musical arranging and general studio direction were much better than just sitting there and being told what to do. I'd been doing some sessions with Donovan. The first thing I really did with him was 'Sunshine Superman'. I happened to be on the session as a bass player and I ended up doing the arrangements. The arranger they'd

picked for the session really didn't know about anything. I got the rhythm section together and we went from there."

He became musical director for Mickie Most which, among many other tasks, involved working with The Yardbirds on several songs for the 'Little Games' album. This renewed his acquaintance with Jimmy Page, who he had met on numerous sessions in the past.

By the summer of 1968, John Paul Jones was highly respected by fellow musicians though completely unknown to the public, and presumably he was making a good living. But this isn't the be all and end all, even for a married man with two young daughters, and he was on the lookout for a new challenge. He very nearly joined Terry Reid's new band, but then he heard that Jimmy Page was putting a new group together.

Page recalls: "I was working at the sessions for Donovan's 'Hurdy Gurdy Man' and John Paul Jones was looking after the musical arrangements. During a break he asked me if I could use a bass player in the new group I was forming. Now John Paul Jones is unquestionably an incredible arranger and musician – he didn't need me for a job. It was just that he felt the need to express himself and he thought we might be able to do it together. He had a proper musical training and he had quite brilliant ideas. I jumped at the chance of getting him."

Robert Plant

Born Robert Anthony Plant on August 20th, 1948, at West Bromwich, Staffordshire. Alone among the members of Led Zeppelin, the young Robert Plant was denied parental encouragement in his musical aspirations. Admittedly, his father did give him lifts to the local blues club in Stourbridge, but as his obsession with the music got stronger and his hair got longer, relations became increasingly strained.

The situation reached a climax when Plant left school in the summer of 1964, having acquired 6 'O'-Levels, started a chartered accountancy course and then packed it up within two weeks.

"The decision was the only thing I've ever looked at in my life from a long-term viewpoint. You've just got to have a go at what you really want to do first. I decided that if I didn't get anywhere by the time I was 20, I would pack it in. Of course it didn't really matter what happened because I wouldn't have packed it in anyway. You can't give up something you really believe in for financial reasons.

Fortunately my parents saw it too, but only *after* I'd proved it. Not before. I'm a little sorry about that, actually. They just could not relate to it at all, not even on a musical level. I just wasn't toeing any normal line."

So, at the tender age of 16, Plant left home and went to live in Walsall. He played in numerous Midlands bands, including The Crawling King Snakes (with John Bonham), Black Snake Moan and The Delta Blues Band. As the names suggest, most of these out-

fits were blues bands, but his influences and style expanded considerably as he started listening to the groups coming out of America's West Coast from 1966 onwards.

Like John Bonham, Plant established a local reputation and virtually starved. For much of the time, he was kept by his girlfriend Maureen, whom he had met at a Georgie Fame concert in 1966, and at one point he even turned his hand to road-making to keep the wolf from the door.

He did manage to get a solo contract with CBS and released two singles during 1967, 'Our Song/Laughing, Crying, Laughing' and 'Long Time Coming/I've Got A Secret'. Neither set the world alight, however, so it was back to the Midlands and The Band of Joy.

The Band of Joy are now the group which everyone associates with Plant and Bonham in their pre-Zeppelin days, but no-one was terribly interested in them at the time.

John Bonham

Born John Henry Bonham on May 31st, 1948, at Redditch, Worcestershire. It seems John Bonham was destined to be a drummer almost from birth. In his very early youth, he used to beat on his mum's pots and pans. Then he adapted bath salt containers and coffee tins with wire attachments before being given a proper snare drum when he was 10. By the time he was given his first full drum kit, when he was 15½, he had already decided where his future lay.

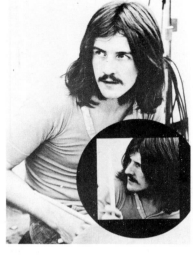

parents stuck by me."

Someone else who stuck by him in his ambitions was his wife Pat, whom he met at a dance and married at the tender age of 17. The couple lived in a small caravan, and at one point things were so bad that Bonham had to give up smoking to pay the rent.

On the bright side, his work with local bands around the Birmingham area, like Terry and The Spiders and A Way Of Life, was getting him something of a reputation. It also got him banned by several club managers, who felt his playing was too violent for the delicate ears of their customers.

For a short while Bonham played with The Crawling King Snakes who had a singer by the name of Robert Plant, and after spells with The Nicky James Movement and Steve Brett & The Mavericks, the two met up again in The Band of Joy.

"When I left school I went into the trade with my Dad. He had a building business and I used to like it. But drumming was the only thing I was any good at, and I stuck at that for three or four years. If things got bad I could always go back to building.

I was so keen to play when I left school, I'd have played for nothing. In fact I did for a long time, but my

Nevertheless, they did enable Robert to travel down to London, where Alexis Korner, one of the grand old men of British R&B, spotted him at a Speakeasy gig. "I rather liked Robert", he relates, "and since The Band of Joy disintegrated a couple of gigs later, we worked out a loose arrangement and did some gigs around the Birmingham area. We started an album that was never finished. One of the tracks, 'Operator', came out on an album called 'Bootleg Him'... We worked on and off for a year but it was all very loose – I just didn't want to re-form a band at that time. Robert needed a regular sum of money. It wasn't a lot, but it

was more than I could afford. So he was looking around."

Plant's search took him to Tony Secunda, the manager of The Move, another Birmingham area band. Secunda tried to get him signed by Regal Zonophone, who were enjoying a lot of success with Procol Harum and Joe Cocker, but although label boss Denny Cordell liked him, he was too busy to sign any more acts.

So Plant went back to the Midlands yet again and played odd dates with local bands, little suspecting that fate was about to lend a very large hand.

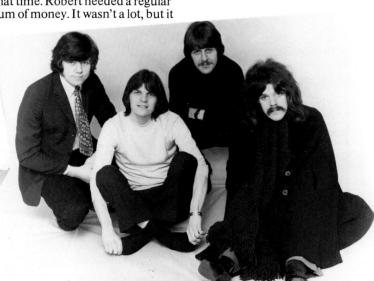

Peter Grant

The incredible, chequered career of Peter Grant, the "fifth member" of Led Zeppelin and the most celebrated manager since Brian Epstein, is probably best recapped by the man himself:

"I had a bad, bad education . . . it was all mixed up with being evacuated during the war and my circumstances . . . I don't remember father, but I have a marvellous mother, who I've been able to look after really well now.

When I was 13 I became a stage hand at the Empire, Croydon theatre in London. I also tried working in a sheet metal factory, but after only five weeks I knew it just wasn't in me. Then I got a job at Reuters, taking photos round Fleet Street . . . I ran around to the customers with wet pictures hanging over my arms. I was also employed as a waiter.

Then came National Service in the RAOC. I became corporal in charge of the dining hall. I enjoyed my time there because it was a very cushy number. I worked a season at a holiday camp, which was dreadful. Then I stinted for a time as entertainment manager at a hotel in Jersey. Then back to London to work in a Soho coffee bar – Tommy Steele was discovered there. Mickie Most was a waiter and I was on the door . . . they paid us 10 shillings and a meal a night. Being doorman at Murray's Cabaret Club was good fun too – I wasn't married then, and what with me being the only man around and about 40 girls backstage, it was all right.

This venture lasted about a couple of years until early 1968, during which time the group released three singles, went through several changes of musical direction, and toured the country supporting American singer-songwriter Tim Rose. Robert Plant recalls: "Eventually we were getting between 60 and 75 quid a night. But it didn't keep improving. In the end I just had to give it up. I thought 'Bollocks; nobody at all wants to know about us'."

When The Band of Joy broke up, Bonham accepted an offer to join

Tim Rose's backing group for another British tour, and for the first time in his career he was earning regular money . . . albeit only £40 a week.

By now his fame in musicians circles was such that he was being sought by Chris Farlowe and Joe Cocker, both fairly tempting positions at the time, when Robert Plant crossed his path yet again, with a proposition that was to increase his standard of living even more dramatically.

I was also a wrestler for about 18 months when I needed some money, and then I got into acting. I doubled for Robert Morley in films and took on small parts in the TV series 'Dixon of Dock Green' and the Sid James/Tony Hancock series. I even played in the box office record breaker 'The Guns Of Navarone', but filming's not for me. Getting up at 6am and flogging it down to Pinewood Studios or somewhere – it's too much.

I was invited to be tour manager for several early American rock acts – Gene Vincent, Little Richard and Jerry Lee Lewis. After that I started managing, more by chance than anything else ... I was finishing off working for an agent and I heard a group in Newcastle called The Alan Price R&B Combo, and eventually I managed them and later they became The Animals.

I just kinda came around to it. With all the odd jobs I'd done, it just gravitated that way. You don't just wake up in the morning having been a salesman or a dentist and say 'Hey, I'm going to manage groups'. You've got to move around the show business scene, and that I think I've done."

Record producer Mickie Most was also involved with The Animals, and in 1964 the two men formed RAK Music Management.

"RAK was chosen as the name of the company, but names are not important in this business. People don't say 'Let's get in touch with RAK Management', they say 'Let's go see Peter Grant'. It was the same with the late Brian Epstein. Who'd ever heard of NEMS, his company? It was always 'Let's contact old Brian'. I think that people nowadays spend too much time and energy on finding names and making their premises swell. Why bother? It's the personal bit that matters. At one point, Mickie Most and myself and three girls worked in these offices, and we had four LPs in the Top Twenty. At that point I also managed Jeff Beck and Terry Reid, and I had a business interest in Donovan. So why should I sweat it out to look ritzy?"

Eventually, Grant gave up all his other activities to look after Led Zeppelin, but his basic style never changed. His various offices were always unassuming, and his

personal appearance was highly unconventional at a time when most managers came on like suave business executives (at the peak of Zeppelin's fame it was rumoured that he didn't even own a suit). Yet

few people would dispute that Peter Grant's record, with other artists as well as Zeppelin, makes him probably the most effective manager in the history of rock music.

1968

August 1968

Left with The Yardbirds name, the support and counsel of Peter Grant, and a head full of ideas, Jimmy Page retreated to his converted Victorian boathouse by the Thames at Pangbourne, in Berkshire, to think things over.

The news that he was planning to form a new group spread quickly on the musicians' grapevine, and before long he got a call from John Paul Jones. Jones, like Page himself two years earlier, was eager to get away from the session scene. And Page, well acquainted with Jones' talents as an instrumentalist and arranger, was just as eager to have him.

First choices for the positions of vocalist and drummer were Terry Reid, whom Page had admired with Peter Jay and The Jaywalkers, and B.J. Wilson, Procol Harum's drummer.

Both were unavailable, but Reid was able to recommend another young vocalist called Robert Plant, who had recently been down in London looking for a break.

Page and Grant travelled up to Birmingham to see him play at a teacher training college with his band, Hobbstweedle. They were suitably impressed and, after a few days at Pangbourne, Plant was in too.

He in his turn recommended John Bonham, but as Bonham was on tour with Tim Rose, getting hold of this last piece of the jigsaw proved rather difficult. Finally, Plant caught up with him in Oxford and discovered he wasn't the only one after the drummer's services.

John Bonham: Joe Cocker was interested and so was Chris Farlowe, along with Robert and Jimmy. It was baffling. I had so much to consider ... When I first got offered the job, I thought The Yardbirds were finished because in England they had been forgotten. Still, I thought 'Well, I've got nothing anyway, so anything is really better than nothing'. I knew that Jimmy was a good guitarist and I knew that Robert was a good vocalist, so even if we didn't have any success it would at least be a pleasure to play in a good group. I already knew what Robert liked and Jimmy told me what he was into, and I decided I liked their music better than either Farlowe's or Cocker's.

Even with Bonham's agreement, however, the problems weren't over. His home didn't have a telephone, and no fewer than 40 telegrams had to be dispatched from Grant's office before he could be summoned to begin work.

September 1968

Rehearsals began at Page's London flat, with the group working on a repertoire of new tunes, old blues and R&B numbers, and a couple of songs from The Yardbirds days. One of these, 'Train Kept A'Rollin,' which has never appeared on a Zeppelin album though often played on stage, was apparently the first song they ever played together.

Things went sensationally right from the word go. Plant recalls: "You just couldn't walk away and forget it. The sound was so great". Which was just as well, because within three weeks of meeting, the group was en route to its first date in Copenhagen, at the start of a 10-day Scandinavian tour.

This tour, and a few early gigs in England, were done as The New Yardbirds to fulfil old contractual obligations. But the group's real name had already been decided.

The precise origin of the Led Zeppelin name has become a cause of slight controversy.

John Entwistle: There were several occasions with The Who when both Keith Moon and myself were going to leave the band. Once when we were in New York, I sat down with Keith and our chauffeur, a guy called Richard Cole, and tried to come up with possible new names for the band we were going to form. That's when I flashed on Led Zeppelin, and I also came up with an idea for a first album jacket with a Zeppelin going down in flames.

Not long afterwards Richard Cole, the chauffeur, went to work for Jimmy Page and Peter Grant and he must have told them the idea. But I was definitely the one who thought of it. Later on Keith Moon claimed that he came up with it, which made me very angry. When I heard Jimmy was going to use it, I was a bit pissed off about it, but later on I didn't care that much.

Jimmy Page: Well, I don't know about that at all ... to start with, the thing about the cover is completely wrong. We did that quite separately. The other — well, Keith Moon gave us the name. We've always credited him with that. Maybe John Entwistle did think of the name and told it to Keith Moon, in which case I suppose he might have cause to be a bit angry.

Whoever had the original idea, though, it began as Lead Zeppelin, and only got shortened when Peter Grant realised that punters, especially across the Atlantic, might mispronounce it.

October 1968

Back from Scandinavia, the band went into Olympic Studios at Barnes, South London, to record their début album. Recorded in 30 hours, it cost a mere £1,782 (including the cover) and by 1975 would gross £3,500,000.

Jimmy Page: It was easy because we had a repertoire of numbers all worked out and we just went into the studio and did it. I suppose it was the fact that we were confident and prepared which made things flow smoothly in the studio, and — as it happened — we recorded the songs almost exactly as we'd been doing them live. Only 'Babe I'm Gonna Leave You' was altered, as far as I can remember ... it was partly an attitude of 'let's get the job done and not mess about having a party in there', but it certainly wasn't a first take effort. We went on until we were happy with each number.

Page was producer, a task for which he was well prepared by his years of watching Britain's top producers at work. And seven of the nine songs were credited to various members of the group, although Robert Plant's name doesn't appear as a writer because he had a publishing contract elsewhere.

15

The world début of Led Zeppelin at Surrey University.

18

The UK début of The New Yardbirds at the Marquee.

John Gee (Marquee manager): Their manager, Peter Grant, was really all geared up before the gig. He told me this was going to be a fantastic new group. He really had a lot of faith in them. But the group was very loud ... I thought they were overpoweringly loud for the size of the Marquee. It might have been all right in one of those massive American stadiums, but it was too loud for the Marquee. Anyway, the lads received an enthusiastic but not overwhelming response from the audience.

19

The New Yardbirds' last date at Liverpool University.

While this was going on, Page was still doing occasional sessions, including Al Stewart's 'Love Chronicles' and Joe Cocker's 'With A Little Help From My Friends'. It was quite important that he did, as he was having to subsidise the others in the early days, but before long the spare time for such extramural activities would become very limited indeed.

November 1968

9
The London début of Led Zeppelin at the Middle Earth club, held at the Chalk Farm Roundhouse. They got £150 and two standing ovations.

Earlier that day, Robert Plant got married to Maureen. Later that month, she gave birth to their first child, Carmen Jane.

16
Manchester College of Science and Technology.

23
Sheffield University.

Between gigs, Peter Grant set off for New York, carrying live tapes, album tapes and the sleeve artwork, with the aim of securing a worldwide deal. He got one. Not with Epic, the subsidiary of Columbia who had rights to The Yardbirds in the States, but with Atlantic.

Dick Asher (Columbia executive): **We at Columbia felt that Epic had done a really good job in promoting The Yardbirds ... We thought we'd done very well on Jimmy Page. When we heard that The Yardbirds had split up and Jimmy Page had formed Led Zeppelin, we naturally assumed that the rights to Page would go automatically to Columbia, the other three being subject to mutual agreement ...**

So Grant and Weiss (Zeppelin's attorney) duly arrived in Clive's office (Clive Davis, President of Columbia) and we all sat down. It was Clive's first meeting with Peter Grant and we talked and talked and talked about all sorts of things. It just went on and on but there was no mention of Led Zeppelin. Finally Clive said: 'Well,

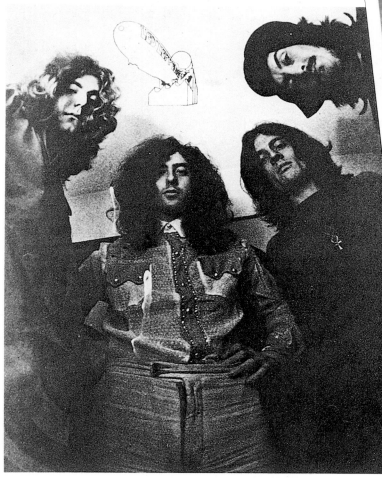

aren't we going to talk about Jimmy Page?' Grant replied 'Oh no, we've already signed the Zeppelin to Atlantic'. Grant explained that Jimmy Page had never been signed as an individual, only as part of The Yardbirds group

Clive just went berserk ... and I think with some justification. The Yardbirds had been one of his pet projects. We were all stunned – especially after all we had done for the group.

The five-year contract which Grant had negotiated with Atlantic included a rumoured advance of

$200,000. This was the highest ever paid to a new group, and a quite astonishing sum, considering the record company had never seen them.

Perhaps more important, however, was the unprecedented degree of independence that Grant won for his charges. Having set up production and publishing companies a few weeks previously, they were now responsible for every creative aspect of their career, from record production right through to publicity pictures.

When the rest of the music business found out about it, it started a small revolution in company/artist relations.

Jimmy Page: **You can develop a tremendous insecurity if your management isn't totally reliable. I know that money is a dirty word in this business, but the fact remains that if you have any measure of record success, you're going to have royalties coming in. Many groups who have been working for years and years end up with nothing because they've been screwed all the way down the line. That sort of thing is heartbreaking. We're very lucky in that respect because we've got Peter Grant, who is like a fifth member of the group.**

December 1968

10
Marquee, London.

16
Bath Pavilion for £75.

19
Exeter City Hall for £125.

20
Fishmongers Hall, Wood Green, London.

Peter Grant: **Before we got the LP, we couldn't get work here in Britain. It seemed to be a laugh to people that we were getting the group together and working the way we were. I don't want to name the people who put us down and thought we were wasting our time, but there were plenty of them.**

Jimmy Page: **It was just a joke in England. We really had a bad time. They just wouldn't accept anything new. It had to be The New Yardbirds, not Led Zeppelin. We were given a chance in America.**

26
Led Zeppelin's US début in Denver, Colorado.

28
Boston Tea Party, supporting Vanilla Fudge and MC5.

John Paul Jones: **We played for hours, and we only had an hour and a half act, so if anyone knew more than four bars of any tune, we would go into it. We did old Beatles numbers and Chuck Berry numbers. It was the greatest night. We knew that we had definitely done it by then.**

1969

January 1969

Zeppelin's first American tour, arranged by Premier Talent, the top rock agency in the States at that time, was carefully planned to make maximum impact.

From touring with The Yardbirds, The Animals and others, Peter Grant knew which cities and which gigs would be most helpful in breaking the band. Special emphasis was given to dates on the West Coast, where The Yardbirds had enjoyed a particularly strong following.

9, 10, 11

Fillmore West, San Francisco supporting Country Joe & The Fish.

Jimmy Page: I can tell you when I knew we'd broken through . . . San Francisco. There were other gigs, like the Boston Tea Party and the Kinetic Circus in Chicago, which have unfortunately disappeared as venues, where the response was so incredible we knew we'd made our impression. But after the San Francisco gig it was just – bang!

While the band toured, Atlantic built up a promotion campaign around them, distributing white label pressings of the album to radio stations and the press. By the time it was released, advance orders had reached 50,000.

17

'Led Zeppelin' released in the USA to a mixed critical reception.

John Mendelsohn (Rolling Stone): It would seem that if they're to fill the void created by Cream, they will have to find a producer, editor and some material worthy of their collective talents.

Ritchie Yorke (Toronto Globe and Mail): The best début album by any group since 'Are You Experienced'.

With no single off the album and limited airplay outside areas like San Francisco, where the Zeppelin name already meant something, the only way for the band to get noticed was through live work. So that's the way they did it.

Jimmy Page: We started off at less than $1500 a night. We played for only $200 at one gig, but it was worth it. We didn't care. We just wanted to come over to America and play our music. I had assumed that even though The Yardbirds had been getting about $2500 a night, Led Zeppelin could only hope to start off at about the $1500 mark and work our way up from there.

31

Fillmore East, New York, supporting Iron Butterfly.

February 1969

1

Fillmore East, New York. After these two nights, Zeppelin had cracked it on the East Coast, as well as the West Coast. Iron Butterfly

were undoubtedly the biggest heavy band in the country at the time, with 'In-A-Gadda-Da-Vida' well on its way to becoming the first ever platinum rock album.

But Zeppelin outshone them to such an extent that, so the rumours ran, they were almost literally destroyed by it. Certainly Iron Butterfly started drifting into oblivion thereafter, while Zeppelin soared.

John Paul Jones: The Americans had it their own way for so long. As soon as some competition comes along and succeeds, the not-so-good American bands get uptight because they think they're missing out on all the work. The better bands just pull their fingers out and come up with something really great. Then they do as well as the English bands.

Gradually the album was picking up sales, as the group's live performances reached more people and the good word spread. In mid-February, it entered the Billboard charts at 99, rising rapidly to 40 and then to 28. It finally peaked during May at No. 10, and went on to spend 73 consecutive weeks in the Top Hundred.

By the time Zeppelin flew home

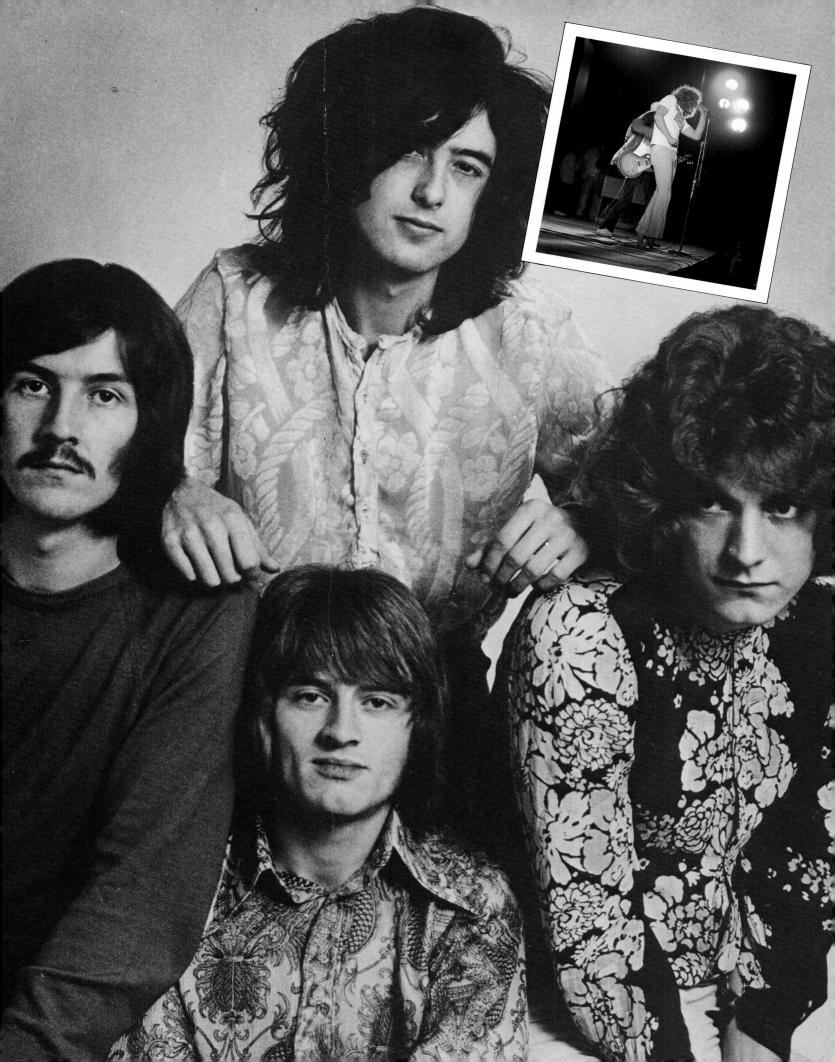

LED ZEPPELIN
Authentic arrangements! · The complete album featuring
photos, biographies and tips to players by
JIMMY PAGE, JOHN PAUL JONES, JOHN BONHAM and ROBERT PLANT
EXTRA special guitar arrangement of BLACK MOUNTAIN SIDE

VOCAL
PIANO
GUITAR
ORGAN
BASS

WARNER BROS. MUSIC

$2.95

carried on home turf.

Most of the dates were in small clubs, but they did at least reach right across the country, from Plymouth to Stoke and from Cardiff to Sunderland, and the London area was very comprehensively covered.

15

A break in the UK schedule for a short Scandinavian tour.

21

Led Zeppelin's first (and only) UK television appearance, on the late night show 'How It Is'. Coming in as last minute replacements for The Flying Burrito Brothers, they performed 'Communication Breakdown'.

While Zeppelin trekked round the country, 'Led Zeppelin' finally got released in the UK. Unlike in the States, where the critics had been divided over the album's

at the end of the month, they knew that the decision to concentrate their efforts in America had paid off beyond their wildest dreams.

June Harris (New Musical Express): **The biggest happening of the 1969 heavy rock scene is Led Zeppelin! The reaction to the group's first tour here, currently in process, has not only been incredible, it's been nothing short of sensational.**

Jimmy Page: **I think what did it for us was the stage thing. We came here unknown on that first tour, we did our number and the word got out that we were worth seeing. We tried as hard as we could on stage and it worked. Before they saw us in America there was a blast of publicity and they heard all about the money being advanced to us by the record company. So the reaction was 'Ah, a capitalist group'. They realised we weren't when they saw us playing a non-stop three-hour show every night.**

March 1969

Back in Britain, it was almost back to square one. Some news of the band's triumphal progress through America had filtered back via the music press, but generally interest was low.

Grant had set up an 18 date tour, running from early March to mid-April and the fees, which varied from £60 against 60% of the gross to a maximum of £140, give some idea of the weight the Zeppelin name

merits, reaction in the British papers was almost unanimously favourable.

Felix Dennis (Oz): Very occasionally, an LP record is released that defies immediate categorisation, simply because it's so obviously a turning point in rock music that only time proves capable of shifting it into eventual perspective. This Led Zeppelin album is like that.

Chris Welch (Punch): The definitive recorded rock performance of the year.

22
Birmingham, Mother's.

28
London, Marquee.

30
Potter's Bar, Farx

April 1969

1
Hampstead, Klooks Kleek.

5
London, Chalk Farm Roundhouse.

8
Welwyn Garden City, Cherry Tree.

12
Tolworth, Toby Jug.

When the tour finished on April 17th, the album was already firmly entrenched in the Top Ten and would be on the charts for 22 successive weeks. Britain had fallen even more easily than America.

Jimmy Page: It's amazing. We're working every day now, but before we went to America hardly anyone wanted to know. And it's not just London . . . it's all over England. Very pleasing reaction. I still reckon the States is our main market, though. It's so very big. It's not that I'm opposed to working in England — far from it — people got that impression with The Yardbirds, but it's not that. The thing is that we can get exposure in America, whereas in England it's all so different. It's too limited. There's only John Peel's or Pete Drummond's radio shows for exposure.

20
Led Zeppelin fly back to the States.

24
The second American tour opens at the Fillmore West.

Not surprisingly, Zeppelin went back to America as bill toppers, playing many of the places where they had originally appeared as a support act, and earning four times their original fees. For much of the tour, they were supported by Julie Driscoll and The Brian Augur Trinity.

The group's set, which now ran to about two hours, opened with 'Train Kept A'Rollin'' and featured a Jimmy Page acoustic spot, on 'White Summer' and 'Black Mountain Side', and a rock 'n' roll medley as an encore.

May 1969

After a string of dates in the San Francisco area, Zeppelin moved down to Los Angeles and then rolled across the continent, leaving ecstatic audiences everywhere in their wake.

As well as building their musical reputation, Zeppelin were also developing a reputation for off-stage activities. While staying at the Hyatt House in Los Angeles, the delivery of Jimmy Page on a room service trolley to a bedroom full of girls was apparently among the least of their high jinks.

Robert Plant: Most of the girls who come backstage simply want to say 'Thank you' to us for giving a good concert. Outsiders who think that all sorts of stuff is going on just don't know us. I'll admit the first year or two that I became a star, I was very young and was on a sort of trip. But we've gotten over all that now.

17

'Led Zeppelin' enters the Billboard Top Ten.

30, 31

The second American tour ends at the Fillmore East, where Zeppelin are supported by Woody Herman and Delaney & Bonnie.

Robert Plant: I think that on the second tour, people really started taking an interest in the other members of the group and not just Jimmy. Each of us has a different personality which is now coming to the fore.

The tour had been another astonishing success, and the band were now firmly established as one of the biggest live attractions in rock. But the critics still disagreed over them.

Variety: This quartet's obsession with power, volume and melodramatic theatrics, leaves little room for the subtlety the other Britishers employ. There is plenty of room for dynamics and understatement in the Zeppelin brand of ultra-hard rock. But the combo has forsaken their musical sense for the sheer power that entices their predominantly juvenile following.

World Convention: They are recognised as the best blues-oriented group around, and that's some accomplishment, considering the fiercely competitive group scene today . . . Led Zeppelin has succeeded in fusing musicianship and showmanship to produce one of the most unusual and exciting stage performances ever.

June 1969

Zeppelin had returned home from their first American jaunt to find themselves almost ignored. How things had changed in a few short months. Now Britain couldn't get enough of them. Zeppelin were the new heroes of the British rock scene, and they promptly embarked on a busy schedule of live dates and radio appearances to enhance that position.

13

Birmingham Town Hall.

15

Manchester Free Trade Hall.

16

Radio One, David Symonds Show.

20

Newcastle City Hall.

21

Bristol, Colston Hall.

23

Radio One, Top Gear.

26

Plymouth, Guildhall.

27

Radio One, hour-long LZ special, recorded at London's Playhouse Theatre.

28

Bath Festival of Blues and Progressive Music. Zeppelin's biggest gig yet in the UK, where they were seen by 12,000 fans.

29

London, Royal Albert Hall. The first night of the Pop Proms series.

Nick Logan (New Musical Express): The Zeppelin truly deserve the acclaim — it is boggling that in a matter of months they have achieved such a high degree of musicianship and become one of the biggest crowd pullers around.

When the houselights turned off at 11pm, after one encore, the group returned to the stage to play 'Long Tall Sally', with the saxists from Liverpool Scene and Blodwyn Pig, with the audience on their feet and dancing and a ticker tape reception of hand bills and balloons and petals of flowers from the foot of the stage.

July 1969

5

Zeppelin fly to the States for their third tour, which would see them move up the scale yet again, from the major halls to sports arenas and stadia, and big open air festivals.

6

Newport Jazz Festival.

11

Baltimore Jazz Festival.

12

Philadelphia Jazz Festival.

For the big American jazz festivals to open their arms to rock groups was something very new. But the

Plant found himself putting the vocals on 'Bring It On Home' in a studio that was little more than a shed.

Jimmy Page: **The album took such a long time to make . . . it was all on and off. It was quite insane, really. We had no time and we had to write numbers in hotel rooms. By the time the album came out, I was really fed up with it. I'd just heard it so many times in so many places. I really think I lost confidence in it. Even though people were saying it was great, I wasn't convinced myself.**

31

The third American tour ends with a performance at the Dallas Festival, for which Zeppelin received $13,000.

September 1969

For the first time in nearly a year, the group took time out for a few weeks. Bonham, Plant and Jones retreated to their country homes to spend time with their families. Page and his girlfriend Charlotte went off for a holiday in Spain and Morocco.

On his return, he finished work on the new album at Olympic Studios, where it had begun several months before.

Jimmy Page: **I do worry that the second album is turning out so different from the first. We may have overstepped the mark. But then again, I suppose there are enough Led Zeppelin trademarks in there. It's very hard rock, no doubt about that. There aren't many bands into hard rock these days and I think that might account for some of our success. All sorts of people are into folk, country and soft stuff. We just like to play it hard and bluesy.**

festivals needed the new audiences that the groups would attract. And the groups (who included Jeff Beck and Ten Years After, as well as Zeppelin) got the chance to play to a large crowd and pick up a large pay packet.

13

Singer Bowl. This gig culminated in a mighty jam session, with Bonham, Plant and Page joined by Jeff Beck, Rod Stewart, Glenn Cornick from Jethro Tull and Rick Lee from Ten Years After, for a workout on 'Jailhouse Rock'.

21

New York, Central Park. Part of the Schaefer Music Festival.

Cashbox: **Led Zeppelin practically brought the house down – no kidding. By the end of a four-encore musical colossus the beam and erector-set framework of the temporary stage (and adjoining walls) were creaking under the strain as performers and audience were swept into a bacchanalia that would have made the most cynical critic wilt.**

For the New York date, 21,000 people had turned up to a venue that held only 10,000. It set the tone for the whole tour, during which 'Led Zeppelin' was certified gold.

In Seattle, they shared the bill with The Doors and repeated the Iron Butterfly treatment.

Seattle Post: **Sunday night was supposed to belong to The Doors. But it was stolen right out from under them by the great English blues group Led Zeppelin.**

August 1969

The third American tour continued, with Cat Mother and The All Night News Boys taking over from Jethro Tull as support band on most of the gigs.

In Los Angeles, where they played the Coliseum, the natives once again went bananas.

Jimmy Page: **America couldn't be better for us at the moment. The scenes there are just incredible. The new system is to put groups on a percentage of the gate money, and we drew 37,000 dollars from one amazing gig in Los Angeles.**

The man largely responsible for this "new system" was, in fact, Peter Grant. Once Zeppelin had reached the top of the tree and could guarantee to sell out virtually any venue around, he introduced a new take-it-or-leave-it deal for promoters. Led Zeppelin would get 90% of the gross. The promoter would pay his expenses and make his profit out of the remaining 10%.

Peter Grant: **The days of the promoter giving a few quid to the**

group as against the money taken on the door is gone. The business was run by managers, agents and promoters, when the funny thing about this business is, it is the groups who bring the people in.

I thought the musicians who bring people in should be the people who get the wages. Now we take the risks. We pay the rent of the hall, we pay the local supporting groups, we pay the promoter to set it up for us.

And that is the way big names are made these days. Not via the press or 'Ready Steady Go', but by people seeing them and making up their own minds.

In their spare time, such as it was, between playing shows, Zeppelin were preparing their second album. Songs were written in hotel rooms and in transit, and recording sessions fitted in on free days. Whenever possible, the band or just Page flew back to New York to use A&R studios there, but on one occasion in Vancouver, Robert

way, they might as well make themselves useful. So they embarked on a swift, three-week campaign, concentrating mainly on the eastern half of the country, which also served to promote the album.

From New York, they went to Detroit, Chicago, Cleveland, Boston (where, ten months after appearing down the bill at the Tea Party, they were paid $45,000 for a night at the Gardens), Buffalo, Providence, Syracuse, Toronto, Kitchener and Kansas City.

22

'Led Zeppelin II' released in the United States. Advance orders for the album had reached 400,000, so it was no surprise that, after entering the chart at 199 in its first week, the album leapt up to 15 and thence to the No. 2 spot. Only 'Abbey Road', the new Beatles album, kept it from the top.

Jimmy Page: **None of us expected to be this big. Frankly, I was surprised when the first album became a gold disc, but I just didn't believe all the people who said our second would do just as well. It was a total shock when I heard that 'LZ II' was actually selling faster than the first one. I just can't believe that they're both now platinum discs. It's really frightening the way it has snowballed . . . especially because it wasn't a contrived thing. It was just good luck and good timing.**

November 1969
6, 7, 8

The fourth US tour ends at San Francisco's Winterland, where Zeppelin are supported by Isaac Hayes and Roland Kirk . . . a typically esoteric Bill Graham presentation.

Once back in England, preliminary work began on the next album (before the second one had even been released in the UK), with just a short interruption for the band's first French appearance, in Paris.

The main event of the month, however, was the release of Zeppelin's first American single.

This was an edited version of 'Whole Lotta Love', which lost 2 of its original 5½ minutes length to satisfy the demands of American radio programmers.

Billboard: **The hot LP sellers make a strong bid for the singles market with this powerful, commercial swinger that should have no trouble putting them up the Hot 100.**

Indeed it didn't. The single entered the Billboard chart at 91 and eventually reached No. 4 at the end of January 1970. The group were not amused, however, despite the record's success.

In the 'Melody Maker' readers poll, Led Zeppelin were voted 3rd in the Brightest Hope category. The fact that this result should seem so ludicrous only a few weeks after the vote was taken, demonstrated graphically how far and how fast the group had progressed by the end of their first year together.

October 1969

The month started quietly, as the four members of Led Zeppelin made the most of their well-earned rest. But things weren't quiet for long.

12

London, Lyceum. This one-off gig was part of a series of Sunday concerts promoted by Tony Smith at the Lyceum Ballroom in the Strand. For doing it, Zeppelin were paid what was rumoured to be the largest fee ever paid to a group for a single performance in this country.

Rolling Stone: **The concert was an unprecedented success, and the screaming audience proved that it's the music that does it for them, not any hype.**

16

Zeppelin go back to the States for the fourth time in less than a year.

A return visit hadn't been planned quite so early, but an invitation to play at Carnegie Hall was something they couldn't refuse.

17

New York, Carnegie Hall. Zeppelin are the first rock group to play there since the Stones in 1964.

Robert Plant: **It is a big prestige thing, being asked to play there. You have to wait until you're asked to play at the Hall by a committee that runs the place. I don't know why they asked us. Could they think us a nice group?**

Zeppelin obviously decided that, since they were in the States any-

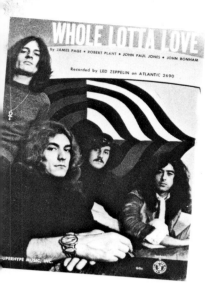

Atlantic in New York and Ahmet could refer to the group's contract which states that Grant has the right to say whether he wants singles out.

And, of course, history has shown that Peter was absolutely right because, at one point, 'LZ II' was selling as fast as a single would sell in those days. The sales really were phenomenal. After a heavy advance sale, it was repeating orders of three, four and five thousand a day, and it went on for weeks selling like that. So I would never again say to Peter Grant that he was wrong about not having singles out with Zeppelin.

Jimmy Page: We just didn't want any of that to happen and we aren't going to be pressurised into things like that any more.

On the positive side, the album had finally been put out in the UK, and was racing to the top of the charts both there and in Europe without any need for a single release.

Phil Carson (Atlantic Records UK chief): I received this phone call from Peter Grant's office telling me that in no way did they want that single out. It was, Peter said, not their policy to put singles out in Britain. I put the phone down and thought to myself 'They're crazy' . . . In the end he convinced me that it shouldn't come out. In his own subtle way, Peter was really insistent. He said that we should call Ahmet Ertegun at

December 1969

11
Mrs. Gwyneth Dunwoody, Parliamentary Secretary to the Board of Trade, presents Zeppelin with one gold and two platinum records for sales of the albums in America. Jimmy Page actually misses the ceremony at the Savoy, having had a small accident on the M4 on the way into London, but consoles himself by purchasing a new Rolls Royce.

27
'Led Zeppelin II' displaces 'Abbey Road' at the top of the Billboard LP chart. It stays there for seven weeks, and will still be on the charts in the spring of 1971.

In the course of 1969, Zeppelin's

expenses had included £24,000 for air fares alone. By way of consolation, they had sold over 100,000 albums in the UK, and over $5 million worth in the United States.

The only bit of bad news was the release of two 'Blues Anthology' albums on Immediate, which included some home recordings that Jimmy had done with Eric Clapton in 1965.

Jimmy Page: That was really a tragedy for me. I got involved with Immediate, producing various things, including John Mayall's 'Witchdoctor', 'Telephone Blues' and a couple of others — and Eric and I got friendly and he came down and we did some recording at home, and Immediate found out that I had tapes of it and said they belonged to them, because I was employed by them. I argued that they couldn't put them out, because they were just variations on blues structures, and in the end we dubbed some other instruments over some of them and they came out — with liner notes attributed to me, though I didn't have anything to do with writing them.

It was just a case of Immediate hustling together whatever they could to fill out the albums, and I'm really embarrassed about the whole thing, because everyone thought I'd instigated it and I hadn't at all.

1970

January 1970

Zeppelin opened the New Year with a short British tour. With John Paul Jones now playing Hammond organ on stage as well as bass, they played for over two hours every night. They didn't take a support act on tour with them, specifically so they could play long sets without running into curfew problems at the halls.

7
Birmingham Town Hall.

8
Bristol, Colston Hall.

9
London, Royal Albert Hall.

13
Portsmouth Guildhall.

15
Newcastle City Hall.

16
Sheffield City Hall.

24
Leeds Town Hall.

Nick Logan (New Musical Express): It isn't hard to understand the substantial appeal of Led Zeppelin. Their current two hour plus act is a blitzkrieg of musically perfected hard rock that combines heavy dramatics with lashings of sex into a formula that can't fail to move the senses and limbs. At the pace they've been setting on their current seven-town British tour there are few groups who could live with them on stage.

February 1970

1
Robert Plant's Jaguar is involved in an accident on the way back from a Spirit concert. He is allowed home after treatment for head and facial injuries, but an Edinburgh date a few days later has to be cancelled.

Jimmy Page: Everything has been slowed up with Robert's accident. That was a horrific scene. The police came banging at the door with flashlights and asked me if I knew a Mr. Robert Plant. When they advised me to

call him at Kidderminster Hospital I knew it had got to be serious. I was really worried, wondering if he had the baby in the car.

He's still in a bad way and we had to cancel some work, although he said he would appear on stage in a wheelchair. He can't lift his arm above his shoulder and he has a cut over his eye.

While Plant recovered, Page kept himself busy, editing tracks for the next album and giving press interviews.

21
Zeppelin begin their first European tour in Copenhagen, billed as The Nobs after threats of legal action from the von Zeppelin family.

Eva von Zeppelin: They may be world famous, but a couple of shrieking monkeys are not going to use a privileged family name without permission.

Jimmy Page: The whole thing is absurd. The first time we played in Copenhagen, she turned up and tried to stop a TV show. She couldn't, of course, but we invited her to meet us to show we were nice young lads. We calmed her down, but on leaving the studio she saw our LP cover of an airship in flames and exploded! I had to run and hide. She just blew her top. So – it's shrieking monkeys now. But she is quite a nice person.

March 1970

12
The end of Zeppelin's European tour.

21
The start of their fifth American tour. The 27 dates scheduled are expected to gross the group $800,000. Fifteen hundred of these are immediately blown on backstage damages at the first gig in Vancouver.

The Zeppelin entourage now includes ten roadies, and eight bodyguards during the Deep South stretch of the tour.

**John Bonham: The restaurant scene in the South can be unbelievable. We've stopped off for a coffee and watched everybody else in the place get service, people who came in after we did. Everybody sits and glares at you, waiting and hoping that you'll explode and a scene will start . . .
We even had a gun pulled on us**

in Texas. Some guy was shouting out and giving us general crap about our hair and all, so we simply gave it back to him. We were leaving after the show, and this same guy turned up at the door. He pulls out this pistol and says to us 'You guys gonna do any shouting now?' We cleared out of there tout de suite.

The group had considered making a documentary of the act for TV during this tour, but eventually decided against it, while still turning down all other offers of TV work.

Jimmy Page: I don't think TV people anywhere know how to present a group, especially from the point of view of getting the right sound. So, if viewers can't see and hear us at our best, then we'd rather stay off the small screen.

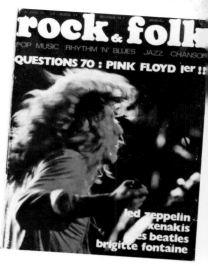

April 1970

6
The members of Led Zeppelin are made honorary citizens of Memphis, Tennessee.

19

The American tour ends in Las Vegas. Robert Plant collapses from exhaustion.

Although the tour had been another triumph, with vast crowds flocking to see Zeppelin in every city they visited, the group had found that America in the spring of 1970 was not the pleasantest place to be.

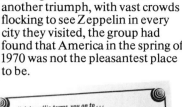

Jimmy Page: **People have no faith in anything. Everyone seems to carry a gun for protection – it's just like being back in the Jesse James era. We had to have armed guards in every car in Georgia. The constant pressure does get to you. But we will go back to the States because people, our audience, want to see us again. I just hope it's cooler next time.**

In Pittsburgh, Pennsylvania, the group had to leave the stage for a short while to help avert violence between police and the audience. But at least the shows were happier occasions in most places.

Back home, despite Zeppelin's reluctance to appear on TV as a group, Jimmy Page did a solo spot on BBC's 'Julie Felix Show', playing his two acoustic showcases from the stage act, 'White Summer' and 'Black Mountain Side'.

May 1970

While Bonham and Jones recovered from the rigours of touring at their respective homes, Page and Plant went off to Wales in search of a little peace and quiet with their families.

Jimmy Page: **We'd been working solidly and thought it was time to have a holiday, or at least to get some time away from the road. Robert suggested going to this cottage in South Wales that he'd been to once with his parents when he was much younger. He was going on about what a beautiful place it was and I became pretty keen to go there. I'd never spent any time at all in Wales but I wanted to. So off we went, taking along our guitars of course. It** wasn't a question of 'let's go and knock out a few songs in the country'. It was just a case of wanting to get away for a bit and have a good time. We took along a couple of our roadies and spent the evenings around log fires, with pokers being plunged into cider and that sort of thing. As the nights wore on, the guitars came out and numbers were being written. It wasn't really planned as a working holiday, but some songs did come out of it.

The cottage by the River Dovey was called Bron-y-Aur, which is Welsh for 'Golden Breat'. Since Page and Plant's visit, it has been immortalised in several Zeppelin numbers and bought by Plant.

Robert Plant: **The great thing about our stay there was that there was no motion, just privacy and nature and the beauty of the people who were there. It was a good experience in every way.**

Once back from Wales, the group booked into Headley Grange, an old country house in Hampshire, for a month's work with a mobile recording studio, beginning on May 19th.

June 1970

The first part of the month was spent at Headley Grange, continuing work on the third Zeppelin album. Then, after a couple of warm-up dates in Iceland, came probably the most important gig Led Zeppelin had ever done.

28

Bath Festival, in front of 200,000 people.

The fact that Zeppelin had turned down offers worth $200,000 to play in Boston and Yale shows how important they felt Bath was. Two hours and five encores later, their decision was justified.

Robert Plant: We knew it was going to be a crucial thing. We went on and knew that the next two or three hours were going to be the ones, as far as holding our heads high. You can still go to the States and earn incredible bread, but that's not what it's all about. I think really we weren't into it until the acoustic number, when we all had a chance to sit down and take

a look around. Then it was like clockwork. We looked at each other and heard it was sounding good, and we looked down and everybody else was grooving too.

Joe Massot (Co-director of 'The Song Remains The Same'): Peter wanted Zep to go on right at sunset, and to make sure of it he physically removed the other group's equipment from the stage. So they did go on just at sunset and it was an amazing experience. With the sun setting behind Robert's hair, the whole gig took on another dimension. The group always felt that Bath was the beginning for them in Britain. They'd sold a lot of

records and played many concerts before, but Bath represented everything falling into place.

July 1970

The only chance for the public to see Led Zeppelin during this month was on a fleeting visit to Germany.

9
Berlin
10
Essen
11
Frankfurt

Zeppelin broke attendance records in all three cities, including the record for the largest-ever audience for a single rock group in Germany, when 11,000 fans crowded into the Frankfurt Festhalle.

Apart from that short break, the group's time was fully taken up with preparing the new album. The third album is often a crucial point in a career, where either new directions and potential, or a rut, begin to develop. Zeppelin were intent on making sure theirs would be the former.

Jimmy Page: I feel that the new album is perhaps the most signifi-

cant of all. We're not changing our policy. It wouldn't be fair if we just *completely* changed our sound and announced we were going to do all new things. On the new album we'll be including some quieter acoustic numbers. But we're still a heavy band.

Robert Plant: The point is that when you begin a new album, you don't know what you'll come up with that might be different. When we conceived the initial numbers at Bron-y-Aur, we started to see what we wanted this album to do. From the start it was obvious it was going to work, and it just grew from there.

I don't think we'll go into a decline just because we've got into some different things. We've already made people aware of us and what we've got to do now is consider the position that we've arrived at . . . so eventually we'll be able to say what we really want to say, and people will listen to it because it's us.

August 1970

5

The sixth American tour begins in Cincinatti. Billed as 'The Greatest Live Event Since The Beatles' and playing without a support act, the minimum fee on this tour was $25,000.

Between dates, mixing on the album was completed, mainly at Ardent Studios in Memphis. On the dates, several of the new numbers were previewed.

As on their earlier American tours, attendances were phenomenal and media coverage minimal. Probably never before or since has an act had such a huge following, while remaining almost entirely unknown outside that following.

September 1970

4

Zeppelin go to Hawaii for a ten day mid-tour break. A couple of gigs on the islands help to pay their way.

19

The tour ends with two concerts at Madison Square Garden, New York. For the first time, Led Zeppelin gross over $100,000 for a performance.

In their absence, a minor sensation had occurred. The 'Melody Maker' National Pop Poll, which had named them Third Brightest Hope 12 months earlier, now announced that Led Zeppelin

had displaced The Beatles as the most popular group in rock music.

They were top group in both the British and International sections, Robert Plant was top British Male Vocalist, 'LZ II' was top British Album, and they took high places in several other categories. Explanations for their success were somewhat diverse.

Melody Maker: **Led Zeppelin's high places are phenomenal but not entirely unexpected. There is no doubt that Zeppelin deserve all their kudos. They have magic, ability and the right attitude in their approach to the business of making music . . .**

They combine the appeal of the traditional pop group format with the excitement, drive and convincing validity of modern rock . . .

There is an excitement about their presence, and careful management has ensured just the right amount of Led Zeppelin is fed to the hungry fans.

L.A. Times: **Their success may be attributable at least in part to the accelerating popularity among the teenage rock 'n' roll audience of barbiturates and amphetamines, drugs that render their users most responsive to crushing volume and ferocious histrionics of the sort Zeppelin has heretofore dealt in exclusively.**

October 1970

5

'Led Zeppelin III' released with 'Led Zeppelin II' still perched at 89 on the Billboard Top 100.

Advance orders of 700,000 in the States and 60,000 in the UK guaranteed the album instant gold status on both sides of the Atlantic, and it dutifully topped charts everywhere. But reviews were generally uncomplimentary, even harsh, and 'Led Zeppelin III' ended up selling notably less well than its predecessor.

Much of this criticism, which attacked the softer elements of the album and accused Zeppelin of jumping on the acoustic bandwagon, completely ignored the fact that their albums and performances had always included such material.

Nevertheless, the group were very upset, particularly since they were so proud of the record, and their already limited intercourse with the press became non-existent.

Jimmy Page: **The third LP did get a real hammering from the press and I really got brought down by it. I thought the album in total was good. But the press didn't like it, and they also went on about this enigma that has blown up around us. I admit we may have made it relatively quickly, but I don't think we overplayed our hand in the press or anything. Yet we were getting all these knocks and we became very dispirited. The**

result was that we left off for almost a year.

On early pressings of the album, the words "Do what thou wilt" were inscribed on the run-off. This was a quote from Aleister Crowley, the English mystic, magician and author, whose life and teachings particularly interested Jimmy Page. Earlier in the year, in fact, Page had bought Boleskine, Crowley's old house on the shores of Loch Ness.

Jimmy Page: **There were two or three owners before Crowley moved into it. It was also a church that was burned to the ground with the congregation in it. And that's the site of the house. Strange things happened in that house that had nothing to do with Crowley. The bad vibes were already there.**

16

Plant, Page and Jones are presented with another batch of gold records by Mr. Anthony Grant (no relation), Parliamentary Secretary to Trade and Industry. The

presentation takes place at a reception held in Atlantic's London offices.

Mr. Anthony Grant: **The government recognises the value of pop groups. Like other exporters, Led Zeppelin are in business, and if they're a success, they deserve a pat on the back.**

November 1970

While Zeppelin relaxed, plans were afoot for a Yardbirds revival.

Jimmy Page: **Giorgio Gomelsky wanted us to do it. He was going to make a film and a record of the performance and, for my part, I said I'd do it if it was done chronologically – a set with Eric on lead, a set with Jeff, then a set with Jeff and me, and finally a set with me, because it obviously wouldn't work with all of us on stage at once. I don't know why it never happened – all I can assume is that somebody wouldn't agree to it.**

21

'Immigrant Song', released as a single in the States, enters the Billboard Hot 100 at 85. Altogether, it will spend 13 weeks on the chart, reaching as high as number 16.

December 1970

Work on the fourth album begins at Island Studios in London.

1971

January 1971

While Peter Grant went off to a health farm to combat his weight problem, the group continued recording.

Jimmy Page: **We started off doing some tracks at the new Island studios in London in December '70, but after that we went to our house, Headley Grange in Hampshire, a place where we frequently rehearse. For some reason, we decided to take The Stones mobile truck there ... because we were used to the place. It was familiar territory. We had even lived there during long rehearsal sessions. It seemed ideal – as soon as we thought of an idea, we put it down on tape.**

'Disc', a British music paper, voted 'Led Zeppelin II' their Album of the Year.

February 1971

Basic recording for the fourth album completed.

Around this time, John Paul Jones was involved in litigation with a gentleman of the same name who was in the singles chart with 'Man From Nazareth'. This resulted in the second JPJ changing his name to John Paul Joans.

20
The first public appearance of all four members in the UK since the Bath Festival, at the 'Disc' awards ceremony.

March 1971

Zeppelin's first British dates since Bath could hardly have been more different from that massive event. Their 'Return To The Clubs' tour was basically a return to many of the places where they had played when they first formed. They played for the original fees, and the punters got in for the original prices.

5
Belfast, Ulster Hall.

6
Dublin, Boxing Stadium.

This was the group's first visit to Ireland, and it took place at a time when most British groups were avoiding the country because of the troubles. It was also the first public airing of 'Black Dog' and 'Stairway To Heaven' from the forthcoming album, which at this point was optimistically scheduled for release some time in April.

Jimmy Page: **It might be called 'Zeppelin IV'. Everybody expects that, but we might change it. We've got all sorts of mad ideas. I was thinking at one time of having four EPs. But we want to keep the price down and frankly, the price of records now is extortionate.**

9
Leeds University.

10
Canterbury University.

11
Southampton University.

13
Bath Pavilion.

14
Hanley.

18
Newcastle, Mayfair.

19
Manchester University.

20
Birmingham, Stepmothers.

21
Nottingham Boat Club.

23
London, Marquee.

June 1971

Mixing on the fourth album almost finished.

Robert Plant: **The intention originally was for a double album, and then we thought 'Well, not this time' – but then we've been saying 'Not this time' since the second album. Jimmy took all the**

It was getting ridiculous. We had noticed when we arrived at the gig that the whole militia was out and I told the promoter 'Look, this is absurd. Either get them out or get them in trim, or there's gonna be a nasty scene'. As if that wasn't enough, the backstage area was totally swamped with people. You could hardly move through it. I told the promoter that if we were going to have this whole squad of militia, he should at least get them to keep the backstage area free of people.

We were still playing in the middle of this cloud of tear gas but it was hopeless, so we said 'Blow this, it's got into tear gas – let's cut it really short'. We did one more number and then we went into 'Whole Lotta Love' and the whole crowd jumped up. By this point there'd been 40 or 50 minutes of tear gas attacks, and finally somebody heaved a bottle at the police. It was not entirely unexpected since the crowd had been getting bombarded for no reason – but of course the moment the bottle went up, that's what the police had been waiting for. Something like 30 or 40 canisters of tear gas were all exploding at once.

Our only way out was through a tunnel and it was filled with tear gas. We had no idea what would be on the other side of the tunnel, but we got through and locked ourselves in our dressing room. All sorts of people were trying to break into the room, probably thinking it was immune from the rest of it. And we'd left the roadies running around trying to save our instruments.

John Paul Jones: The roadies had to be carried off on stretchers, just for trying to save the gear. The police had cordoned off all the audience around the back and

material over to Sunset Sound in Los Angeles with a very famous producer who said it was THE studio, and did the mixes. We finished recording in February and the idea was to mix it there and get it out in March. But he brought the tapes back and they sounded terrible, so we had to start mixing all over again.

Jimmy Page: That's when the fiasco started, because I was pretty confident that it sounded all right to me. In that room it had sounded great, anyway. The trouble was that the speakers were lying. It wasn't the balance, it was the actual sound that was on the tape. When we played it back in England, it sounded like it had gone through this odd process.

July 1971

Zeppelin's annual European tour was marred by the worst riots they would ever experience, at the Vigorelli Stadium in Milan.

Jimmy Page: It was a festival organised and sponsored by the government, and we were playing on the grass in a huge football ground. Five or six other groups went on before us and then we went out and started playing. All

went well for several numbers. Then we suddenly noticed loads of smoke coming from the back of the oval. The promoter came out on stage and told us to tell the kids to stop lighting fires. Like twits we did what he said. We warned the kids that the authorities might make us stop

playing if there were any more fires.

We went on for another 20 or 30 minutes, but every time the audience would stand up for an encore, there'd be loads of smoke. So we just kept on saying repeatedly: 'Stop lighting those fires, please'. But then we suddenly twigged that it wasn't smoke from fires – it was bloody tear gas that the police were firing into the crowd. It wasn't until one canister landed about 20 or 30 feet from the stage and the wind brought it right over to us that we realised what was happening.

there was a big line of policemen holding them there. The only way they could move was forward on to the stage – about 10,000 kids were forced up through the stage. It was a war.

August 1971

19

The start of the seventh American tour in Vancouver. Twenty gigs, all in venues holding at least 12,000 people, will gross over one million dollars for the group.

September 1971

While Zeppelin charged round the USA and Canada, earning their million dollars, The Yardbirds old record company decided to cash in on the group's popularity them-selves. They put out a live album, recorded in New York on March 30th 1968, under the title 'The Yardbirds With Jimmy Page Live At The Anderson Theater', but were forced to withdraw it after only a few days.

Jimmy Page: **If you've ever heard that album, you'll know why we had it stopped. What happened was, Epic said to us 'Can we do a live LP?' and they sent down the head of their light music depart-ment to supervise it. We had an agreement that if the results were good, they could release the album . . . but if not, they'd just file it away.**
Of course, it was terrible. This character who'd been recording

stuff like 'Manuel's Music Of The Mountains' was strictly into muzak, and the concert itself was bad. He'd done things like hanging one mike over the drums so none of the bass drum came through, and he'd miked up a monitor cabinet on my guitar instead of the proper amp through which I was playing all the fuzz and sustained notes . . . so all that was lost and we all knew it was just a joke. But this fellow assured us it would be all right. 'It's amazing what you can do electronically', he said.
Then we went to listen to the master tapes and there were all these bullfight cheers dubbed on it every time there was a solo, and it was just awful. You'd play a solo and then this huge 'RAAH' would come leaping out at you. There was one number where there was supposed to be utter silence in the audience and this guy dubbed in the clinking of glasses and a whole club atmosphere. But we had the right all along to say whether it would be released or not, and made them shelve it.

16

The North American tour ends in Honolulu.

When the tour was over, the band stayed in Hawaii for a short holiday, before embarking on their first visit to Japan.

October 1971

In Japan, Zeppelin did five dates, including a charity performance in Hiroshima, for the victims of the

atom bomb. On one of the dates, Atlantic executive Phil Carson, who was travelling with the group, had to deputise on bass when John Paul Jones fell ill.

John Bonham: **It was just a fan-tastic place to play. Rock music only started to really happen there a few years ago, but it's now the second biggest market in the world. The people were so friendly and we had the best rock promoter in the world there looking after us. It turned out the 'Immigrant Song' is one of our biggest favourites in Japan, and it's the number we always open with. So the audiences were going potty right from the start.**

Less enthusiastic was the response of Japanese hoteliers to Zeppelin's usual off-stage antics. The Tokyo Hilton even banned them for life.

Phil Carson: **The only way of relieving the boredom of this con-stant grind of Hilton hotel rooms is just to have a little bit of fun from time to time. The lads had been playing in America for four weeks and then went straight to Japan for another ten days – they'd been away from their homes for six or seven weeks – things kind of build up and there's a need to let off a bit of steam.**

At the end of the tour, the Zeppelin party made their separate ways home. Grant, Bonham and Jones flew back to England via Moscow, while Plant and Page took their time returning via Hong Kong, Thailand and India.

Robert Plant: **We all bought cameras in Japan and became**

sweaty photographers. Page must have lost about two pounds rushing about taking pictures in the red light district. In Bangkok all the kids followed us calling 'Billy boy, Billy boy', which means queer (because of our hair). But they're laughing and happy all the time.
But it's made us think, because as soon as we landed in Bangkok, the first sign we saw said 'Coming soon, The Marmalade'. They've never heard of us over there, but there's the good old Marmalade going on from there to some-where else exotic.

November 1971

8

The fourth Led Zeppelin album is released. No-one knows quite what to call it, since it carries no title, not even the group's name, just four symbols.

Jimmy Page: **We decided that on the fourth album we would delib-erately play down the group name, and there wouldn't be any information whatsoever on the outer jacket . . . I had to talk like hell to get that done. The record company told us we were com-mitting professional suicide. We said we just wanted to rely purely on the music.**

Robert Plant: **We decided the album couldn't be called 'Led Zeppelin IV', and we were wondering what it should be. Then each of us decided to go away and choose a metaphysical-type symbol which somehow represented each of us individually — be it a state of mind, an opinion, or something we felt strongly about, or whatever. Then we were to come back together and present our symbols.**

What happened, of course, was that almost everybody *did* call it 'Led Zeppelin IV', despite the Zeppelin office sending out copies of the symbols for the press to use.

Reviews were again mixed, though on balance more positive than for 'Led Zeppelin III'. Surprisingly, the album didn't reach Number One in America (about the only country in the civilised world where it didn't), but over the years it has probably been the group's most consistent seller, thanks largely to 'Stairway To Heaven', which was soon to replace 'Whole Lotta Love' as Zeppelin's anthem.

Jimmy Page: **To me, I thought 'Stairway' crystallized the essence of the band. It had everything there and showed the band at its best . . . as a band, as a unit. Not talking about solos or anything, it had everything there . . . It was a milestone for us. Every musician wants to do something of lasting quality, something that will hold up for a long time, and I guess we did it with 'Stairway'.**

To coincide with the album's release, Zeppelin toured Britain

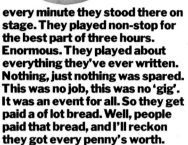

playing most of the major cities, beginning with Newcastle City Hall on November 11th.

20, 21
London, Wembley Empire Pool.

The whole tour had sold out overnight. The two Wembley dates, a total of 19,000 tickets, disappeared in an hour. Thousands of unlucky applicants had to have their money refunded.

Those who were lucky, in return for their 75 pence, saw support bands Bronco and Stone The Crows, various circus performers, and Led Zeppelin at the top of their form.

Roy Hollingworth (Melody Maker): **This was an English band playing like crazy, and enjoying**

every minute they stood there on stage. They played non-stop for the best part of three hours. Enormous. They played about everything they've ever written. Nothing, just nothing was spared. This was no job, this was no 'gig'. It was an event for all. So they get paid a of lot bread. Well, people paid that bread, and I'll reckon they got every penny's worth.

December 1971

2
The British tour ends in Bournemouth.

Reluctantly, the group had agreed to the release of 'Black Dog' as a single in the States. It spent 11 weeks in the Hot 100, with a high of Number 15. This was followed by 'Rock'n'Roll', which was less successful. The group were adamant, however, that 'Stairway' would not be cut down for a single, despite very strong pressure from Atlantic's top brass.

Phil Carson: **Once again, history proved that Peter Grant was right. There had already been two singles off the album, but Atlantic US wanted to revitalise the fourth album prior to the release of the new one, plus the upcoming tour. It was a natural enough move. A lot of AM stations did programme 'Stairway', but it didn't come out as a single . . . so people just bought the album as if it were a single. Which added at least 500,000 copies to the total sale of the album.**

1972

January 1972

By now Page and Jones both had home studios where they could tinker with ideas. The group also got together for occasional sessions at Olympic Studios in London, and Electric Ladyland in New York.

February 1972

14
A date in Singapore, planned en route to a tour of Australasia, has to be cancelled when the members of Zeppelin are refused admission to the country because of their long hair.

16
The Australasian tour opens in Perth. It continues to Adelaide, Melbourne, over to New Zealand to appear before 25,000 people in Auckland, then back to Australia for further shows in Perth, Brisbane and Sydney.

March 1972

4
Sydney Showground, another outdoor concert, attended by 26,000 fans.

10
The end of the Australasian tour.

On the way home, Page and Plant stopped off in Bombay, where they made some experimental recordings with the Bombay Symphony Orchestra.

Jimmy Page: **I heard one guitarist who was really good. I mean he would have held up very easily over here. He played sitar for, what, six years, and he's adapted from that. But it wasn't like raga rock, more like the Mahavishnu.**

He was very good indeed, a very competent musician. He frightened me to death by saying 'Oh, I practise for at least eight hours every day', and you could see that he did, too. He played sort of classical guitar too, but not Bach. Things that were like Bach structures, but his own inventions. But he was getting no market whatsoever, because they didn't understand. They just needed someone to go over and open it up.

April 1972

Karac Plant born.

Recording sessions at Stargroves, Mick Jagger's country home, with The Stones mobile recording studio.

Jimmy Page: **When we went down there, we had no set ideas. We just recorded the ideas each one of us had at that particular time. It was simply a matter of getting together and letting it come out. I don't think we've ever had any shortages or stagnant periods. I've been writing a lot at home and I can try things out in my studio set-up. Lately I've been experimenting with chords a lot more, and unusual voicings. There are several ways in which material can come into the band – but it's always there.**

The sound in the place wasn't as good, recording-wise, as we'd got in that weird place Headley Grange we'd used for the previous album. This was a bit of a deterrent. Nevertheless, we did get quite a bit done – the

immediate stuff that gets laid down right away, even on occasion the vocals.

May 1972

Further recording and mixing sessions at Olympic Studios, London.

June 1972

Overdubbing and mixing sessions at Electric Ladyland, New York.

21

The eighth American tour begins in Denver, Colorado.

By now, Zeppelin sets were running to a minimum of 2½ hours and John Paul Jones was using a whole range of keyboards on stage as well as bass.

John Paul Jones: I'd get bored playing only bass guitar all the time. I'm playing more and more organ onstage now and I want to concentrate on it even more. I don't mind being in the background. I wouldn't like to be out front playing like Jimmy. To be any sort of artist, you have to be a born exhibitionist – I am, but not over anyone else in the business. I believe you should do what you have to do, and if I'm bass, rather than try to lead on bass and push myself, I prefer to put down a good solid bass line.

July 1972

For the members of Zeppelin, this tour of America, which continued through July, was one of their happiest and another sold-out success. But, once again, hardly anyone outside the thousands who saw them play even realised what they were doing.

Roy Hollingworth (Melody Maker): Does anybody really know how big Led Zep are?
So you'll get reports of English

bands doing "well" in America, and the reports will be long. You'll hear The Stones, Elton John and The Faces before you hear of Led Zep. Somehow somebody forgot Led Zeppelin when they were writing home.
And yet for four years Zep have been slaying America. For four years they have met with the dooming criticism that they could never do as well again, and yet they've come back and done better. This present tour will more than likely go down as their best ever. They are playing better than they've ever played in their lives.
The people know it. The scenes are just ridiculous. Auditoriums and halls are being sold out without any advertising. Led Zep are delivering the coup de grâce. Unfortunately it's being overshadowed by The Stones tour, and the garbage that The Moody Blues are the top band. But don't believe it. Led Zeppelin are the ace outfit.

Obviously the group finally thought it was about time the world knew about them too, because after this tour they hired public relations experts for the first time.

Robert Plant: We decided to hire our first publicity firm after we toured here (America) in the summer of '72. That was the same summer that The Stones toured and we knew full well that we were doing more business than them. We were getting better gates in comparison to a lot of people who were constantly glorified in the press. So without getting egocentric, we thought it was time people heard something about us other than that we were eating women and throwing the bones out the window.

It was also after this tour that the group felt forced to cut down a little on the length of their performances, which had been steadily increasing since their first gig.

Jimmy Page: We really had to be mercenary, because the last

American tour got really silly. There were something like 28 dates in 30 days and we were playing an average of three hours per night, sometimes more than that, and it was really doing us in. Now we'll have things from every LP, all the more important tracks. It's really difficult because we really wanted it just to keep on growing, but it became impossible time-wise. You can't introduce four or five new numbers without dropping something.

August 1972

Zeppelin's more open attitude towards the media was immediately seen when they returned to England, as John Bonham took time to give some interviews before heading for a holiday in the South of France.

John Bonham: You get all these letters in the music papers, saying that Led Zeppelin aren't playing and recording any more because they're too busy buying country mansions and Rolls Royces. You know, for a start there ain't one person in this group who owns a Rolls, it must all stem from false information people have read in articles written by people who assume that's what we're doing.

I'm still living in the same bloody house as I was when we first started . . . so's Robert. Nobody's changed that much.
What most people don't understand is that we're always working, even if we don't choose to spread it all over the place. Everyone thinks we're just laying around relaxing, when in fact we are constantly rehearsing and recording. So that puts an end to all that crap, doesn't it?

Perhaps, in the interests of objectivity, it should be pointed out that Jimmy Page had recently acquired an 18th century manor house at Plumpton, Sussex, complete with 50 acres of grounds and lakes. And that Bonham himself, while perhaps not a Rolls Royce owner, in the words of Peter Grant "had more fast cars than anyone else I know. The Birmingham car dealers could survive on him."

October 1972

The second tour of Japan.

28, 29

Montreux Casino, Switzerland. Zeppelin's only European concerts of the year attract fans from all over the Continent.

November 1972

10

Zeppelin's biggest ever British tour, taking in 18 cities, is announced. 120,000 tickets sell out in a day.

The new album is ready, but (as with the previous one) problems with the sleeve artwork are delaying its release.

Jimmy Page: They just couldn't seem to get it right at the printers. The colours are so different from what we anticipated. The basic thing is a photograph in a collage, and then some hand painting . . . we had to compromise because the sky started to look like an ad for Max Factor lipstick, and the children looked as if they'd been turned purple from the cold.

30

The British tour opens at Newcastle City Hall.

Jimmy Page: When you haven't played England for some time, not only do you want things to be spot on, but you always get a little frightened that you'll somehow disappoint the kids. For a first night, the reaction was just tremendous.

December 1972

1
Newcastle City Hall.

3, 4
Glasgow, Green's Playhouse.

7, 8
Manchester, Hardrock.

11, 12
Cardiff, Capitol.

Nick Kent (New Musical Express): Tonight's show has been 'average' – no more, no less, which means that the band got the colossal response they've

registered as a customary reaction over the last few years, culminating in a mammoth rock 'n' roll medley sandwiched in between 'Whole Lotta Love' and three encores.

The set lasted over 2½ hours and was a constant showcase of how dynamics, musical dexterity and sheer drive should be employed when playing hard rock.

16, 17
Birmingham Odeon.

20
Brighton Dome.

22, 23
London, Alexandra Palace.

1973

January 1973

2
Sheffield City Hall.

On their way to start the second leg of the British tour, after the Christmas and New Year break, Plant and Bonham were stranded when their Bentley broke down. They hitchhiked to Sheffield in time for the concert, but Plant acquired a dose of flu in the process and the next two dates had to be postponed.

7
Oxford, New Theatre.

14
Liverpool Empire.

15
Stoke, Trentham Gardens.

16
Aberystwyth, Kings Hall.

Jimmy Page: **We spent a lot of time songwriting in Wales, and Aberystwyth was the nearest large town . . . We felt quite warm vibes about the whole place and so when we set up our last tour we said, wouldn't it be a gas if we did Aberystwyth. Like a nostalgic thing.**

So we did it, but I don't think they could believe we were there because it was a really tiny place, it only held about 800 people, and it was a real folly to do it . . . and they were just aghast. They were all sitting down, it was a corporation type place.

18
Bradford, St. George's Hall, Postponed from January 4th.

21
Southampton, Gaumont.

25
Aberdeen Music Hall.

27
Dundee, Caird Hall.

28
Edinburgh, King's Theatre.

30
Preston Guildhall. Postponed from January 3rd.

March 1973

3
European tour opens in Copenhagen.

4
Gothenburg.

6, 7
Stockholm.

10
Oslo.

13
Munich.

14
Nuremburg.

16
Vienna.

17
Munich.

19
Berlin.

21
Hamburg.

22
Essen.

24
Offenbach.

26
Lyons.

27
Nantes.

29
Marseilles.

31
Lille.

During this tour, the fifth Led Zeppelin album finally emerged, many months overdue. It was titled 'Houses Of The Holy' (apparently a romanticised term for their audiences and the halls which house them), the first time Zeppelin had bothered to give an album a "proper" title.

'Houses Of The Holy' contained little of the heavy blues-rock on which Zeppelin had been founded and a couple of very un-Zeppelin-esque send-ups, 'D'yer Mak'er' and 'The Crunge'. Most critics panned it.

'Rolling Stone' called the album "a dose of pabulum", and even 'Melody Maker' writer Chris Welch, one of the group's staunchest allies, said: "The lack of firm direction is all too apparent. The writing seems to be a compromise between spaced-out ideas and heavy riffs without ever getting to grips with either."

Robert Plant: **So there's some buggers as don't like the album. Well, God bless 'em, I like it and there's a few thousand other buggers like it too.**

Enough other buggers liked it to send 'Houses Of The Holy' to the top of charts all over the world, though it had to wait a couple of months before reaching that coveted spot in the States. Certainly with the benefit of hindsight, it's a much better album than most "experts" allowed, for all its inconsistencies.

April 1973

1, 2
The European tour finishes with two gigs at the Palais des Sports in Paris.

After a break, rehearsals for their forthcoming American tour began at Shepperton Studios. It would be their most massive endeavour yet, and they had prepared themselves accordingly. An American PR firm had been hired to ensure that this time out they wouldn't triumph unnoticed. A private Boeing 720B had been booked to ferry the group members from city to city. Showco, the top rock stage managers in the world, had put together huge sound and lighting rigs, and taken on no fewer than 30 technicians and stagehands to run them. The tour's 33 dates were expected to earn Led Zeppelin something in excess of $4.5 million, and nothing was being left to chance.

Pre-tour inter-office memo: **The following is to be provided in rooms as designated at all hotels in all cities:**
John Bonham – Fresh fruit, beer, champagne on ice, sheep-

skin rug, candles, fresh flowers, milk, fresh orange juice.

Peter Grant – Fresh flowers, champagne on ice, selection of fresh fruit, fresh orange juice, candles.

John Paul Jones – Fresh flowers and fruit (oranges, apples and bananas), bottled Spring water, stereo, piano wherever possible or organ, candles, fresh orange juice.

Jimmy Page – Flowers in bedroom and lounge, fresh fruit (grapes and green apples), bottled Spring water, electric kettle, curtains pulled, candles lit, champagne on ice, fresh orange juice, in bedroom the stereo set to be tuned to a hip FM station.

Robert Plant – Flowers in bedroom, fresh fruit (grapes and lemons), Spring water, Earl Grey tea, tea-making items, fresh orange juice, anything available for food at late hours after gigs.

May 1973

4

The ninth American tour opens at the Atlanta Braves Stadium, in front of 50,000 people.

Sam Cassell (Mayor of Atlanta): **This is the biggest thing to hit Atlanta since 'Gone With The Wind'.**

5

Tampa, Florida. 56,800 fans are at this gig, the largest attendance ever, anywhere, for a performance by a single act.

After this record-breaking start, Zeppelin careered across the Southern States and Texas, before winding up the 18-date first half of the tour in their old stamping ground, California. Despite their threats to shorten sets at the end of the previous American jaunts, the band were still averaging about three hours a night and this time around were featuring a light show and stage effects.

12

'Houses Of The Holy' tops the album charts in America.

30

The first of two dates at the L.A. Forum has to be postponed after Page sprains a finger in an airport fence.

31

L.A. Forum. After this show, a birthday party for John Bonham was held at the Laurel Canyon home of a local radio station owner. Bonham turned up for this event clad in T-shirt, plimsolls and swimming trunks . . . very wisely, as it turned out, since most of the gathering ended up in the swimming pool.

June 1973

2

San Francisco, Kezar Stadium. Another huge gig, seen by nearly 50,000 fans and grossing Zeppelin an estimated $190,000.

Charles Shaar Murray (New Musical Express): **One of the finest musical events I've ever had the privilege to attend. There may be bands who play better, and there may be bands who perform better, and there may be bands who write better songs, but when it comes to welding themselves and an audience together into one unit of total joy, Zeppelin yield to nobody.**

3

L.A. Forum. The rearranged date that had originally been set for May 30th. The conclusion to an astonishingly successful first half.

Steve Rosen (Sounds): **It is surprising that they have done this well. While there are inter-**

mittent flashes of brilliance by Page on guitar and Plant does come up with a worthwhile vocal once in a while, the band is no more than a loud, steel-driven group given to overworked stage gimmicks (smoke machines, flash powder, superstarrish costumes and loud volume).

That the gigs had gone so well (despite the odd cynical critic) was also surprising because Page had been far from well for most of the trip.

Jimmy Page: I still get very ill being on the road. It's probably called malnutrition. I haven't eaten for about three days. You know when you're fasting, after about three or four days you get these pains, and I had one onstage last night – bang. It wouldn't go away . . . I'll probably eat today.

From California, the group went over to Hawaii for a rest. This break came at just the right time, as Page's injured hand was still giving him considerable trouble (he'd had to keep dipping it in cold water during the last three shows) and the holiday gave it a chance to mend.

Jimmy Page: I cut my hand in that area which is crucial for playing the guitar. It was in fact a tendon that was strained – such a stupid thing, really – and in five gigs I fucked it up for five weeks. And I had all manner of treatment and injections.

July 1973

6
The second string of 15 dates begins in Chicago.

For the last few dates of the tour, starting with Baltimore on July 18th and continuing through Pittsburgh and Boston to the climactic three nights in New York, Zeppelin had a film crew along to shoot footage of the shows and surrounding events.

The idea of a Led Zeppelin movie had been in the air for some time, and odd bits and pieces had been filmed to that end, but it wasn' until Joe Massot, a friend of Page's lady Charlotte, got involved that things definitely started taking shape.

Joe Massot: I wanted to represent each one of them as individuals and then incorporate those four sections into a film structure. I told Jimmy that I didn't think there was any point in making another 'Woodstock' or 'Bangla Desh' type of film. They were 16mm documentaries, almost in the home movie style. Even 'Let It Be' fell into that category. There hadn't been a film making any sort of statement about rock or its lifestyle since Dick Lester did 'A Hard Day's Night' and 'Help'. I felt that Jimmy was in the same sort of space about it. He felt the need for something different as well.
Peter called me on July 15 and said 'Come over. We want to make the film'. It was quite a surprise.

27, 28, 29
New York, Madison Square Garden.

Having filmed behind the scenes at the earlier dates, Massot and his crew filmed the show on these three nights. Almost inevitably, the real excitement took place away from the gig.

After the second night, tour

manager Richard Cole and attorney Steve Weiss had put nearly $200,000 in $100 bills into a safe deposit box at the Drake Hotel, ready to pay numerous expenses and wages when the tour ended.

Just before the band set off for the final performance, the box was found to be mysteriously empty. The money was never recovered.

Robert Plant: It was all so ridiculous really. Jimmy and I just laughed about it. I remember Bonzo did go a bit berserk . . . but for Jimmy and I, it all somehow

made sense. There was nothing else you could do but laugh really. Of course, other people not as well endowed as ourselves might draw the conclusion from that that we're mad. But we just laughed.

The big drag of it was the flipout with the media pouring into our bedrooms and taking pictures and asking questions and everything. That sort of reminded us of being knifed or something, and lying in your room getting your last breath while some guy is trying to get it on film

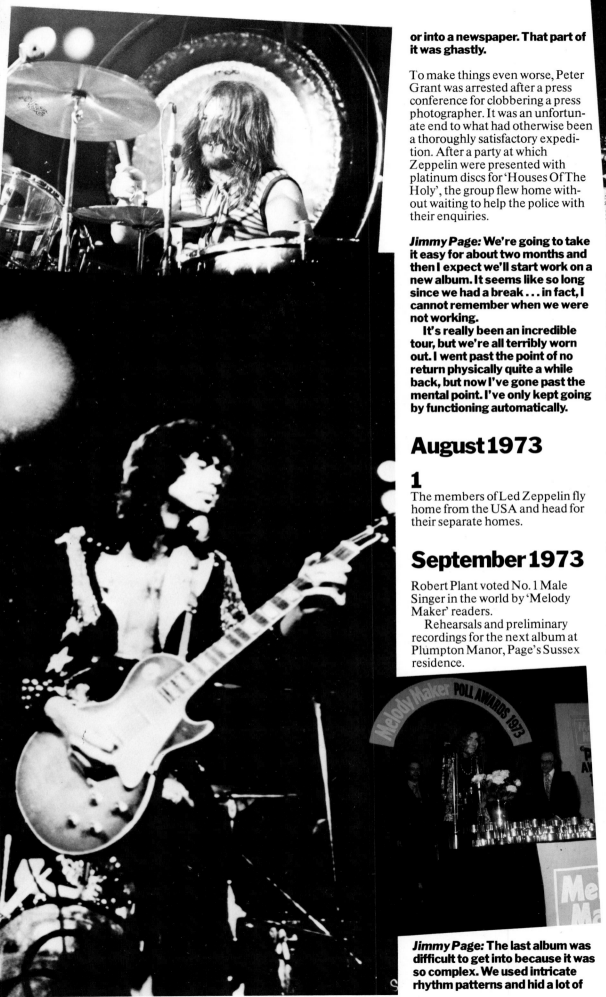

or into a newspaper. That part of it was ghastly.

To make things even worse, Peter Grant was arrested after a press conference for clobbering a press photographer. It was an unfortunate end to what had otherwise been a thoroughly satisfactory expedition. After a party at which Zeppelin were presented with platinum discs for 'Houses Of The Holy', the group flew home without waiting to help the police with their enquiries.

Jimmy Page: **We're going to take it easy for about two months and then I expect we'll start work on a new album. It seems like so long since we had a break . . . in fact, I cannot remember when we were not working.**

It's really been an incredible tour, but we're all terribly worn out. I went past the point of no return physically quite a while back, but now I've gone past the mental point. I've only kept going by functioning automatically.

August 1973

1
The members of Led Zeppelin fly home from the USA and head for their separate homes.

September 1973

Robert Plant voted No. 1 Male Singer in the world by 'Melody Maker' readers.

Rehearsals and preliminary recordings for the next album at Plumpton Manor, Page's Sussex residence.

Jimmy Page: **The last album was difficult to get into because it was so complex. We used intricate rhythm patterns and hid a lot of**

ideas in the lyrics. The next one will still have complex songs, and it'll have an acoustic guitar piece based on a solo I used to do with The Yardbirds during a song called 'White Summer'. But most of the album will get back to something people think we've been drifting away from — straightforward rock 'n' roll.

October 1973

Throughout the autumn, the members of the group had been working on their individual sequences for the planned Led Zeppelin movie. These were shot mainly in the vicinity of their homes. Page's near Boleskine in Scotland; Plant's in Wales, where he now owned a farm, as well as Bron-y-Aur; Bonham's on the Worcestershire farm, which he and his father were building, and at the Santa Pod drag racing track; and Jones's at his home in Sussex.

Joe Massot: **We definitely didn't want just a concert film — we wanted to show them as individuals. But we didn't want to do it in the traditional way, with interviews . . . they felt that they'd like to come up with a more symbolic representation of themselves. In a phrase, these are sequence films of *them*.**

All of the individual sequences were to be integrated into the group's music and concerts. Now the basis of the concert footage is movement, because they perform with such extraordinary movement . . . not just on stage, but within themselves. Zep are a very mobile group. So their individual stories had to have themes of movement as well. I felt this was the key to combining the two. To me the film really took on a lot more interest as I started to do each of the separate stories, because this is where their real characters started to come forth.

John Paul Jones sequence showed him at the head of a band of masked riders, threatening a village, and then returning home to the bosom of his family, removing his mask as he crosses the threshold. Presumably an analogy of his split role as band member and family man – with which Jones always seemed to be slightly uneasy.

John Paul Jones: **Touring makes you a different person, I think. You always realise it when you come home after a tour. It usually takes weeks to recover after living like an animal for so long.**

Plant appeared in his sequence as a cross between a Viking invader and an Arthurian knight on some sort of quest, crossing mountains, battling villains, etc., etc., to find a mysterious lady.

Robert Plant: **Mine wasn't just a role that I was playing, it had some relation to what I consider my role in life. I really do think that life is a journey, and it has its pitfalls and pleasures. But if you ever think that you'll touch that point that you've struggled for . . . well then, life would be a bit flat.**

So consequently, the princess in my sequence, who is the sort of ultimate, disappears. She just vanishes. It would have been too easy for me to have . . . well, gotten it.

For his part, Jimmy Page climbed an alarmingly steep rock face to confront a hooded figure at the summit. This figure is seen to be a very aged Jimmy Page, and in the space of a few seconds regresses to babyhood, then ages again.

Joe Massot: **Jimmy plays both parts in the film. He insisted that his segment be shot on the night of a full moon. It was quite difficult lighting the mountain at night. We actually had to build special scaffolds on the side of it to put the cameras on and mount arc lamps. It was weekend and overtime for the crew but Jimmy wanted it right.**

Jimmy Page: **It hadn't occurred to me, when I was scrambling up the mountain, that I'd have to do about half a dozen takes. Sudden-** ly it hit me that I'd bitten off more than I could chew. In the film it didn't look anywhere near the distance covered – it looked like I was having a promenade.

John Bonham's party piece was the most unassuming of them all, a simple series of scenes of him at home with his wife and son, looning around the countryside with some of his collection of fast motor vehicles, and drag racing.

Joe Massot: **John Bonham chose to be real, just himself. He's sort of a Teddy Boy, playing snooker, riding hot rods a whole exercise in energy and power. He even drives a nitrogen-fuelled dragster at 240mph on a quarter-mile track. The sequence ties in nicely with his drum solo. It's pure power and energy.**

Peter Grant, who had always been acknowledged as a fifth member of the group, got a chance to indulge his fantasies too.

Joe Massot: **We've made two separate films of Peter Grant. One where he is an antique collector, fooling around with vintage cars and driving one around with his wife beside him. Then he's just lying around on a bed fooling with his kids and playing with a cat. It's a very warm film.**
**   The other film, in which Peter plays a gangster in the Al Capone style, has him tearing around in a Pierce Arrow 1928 gangster car in '20s clothes. Richard Cole is dressed up as one of his henchmen, armed with a machine gun. They pull up at this house and machine gun it. I would say it's a stylised dream sequence. But Peter is still uncertain about it. He feels the film might make him look a fool. I don't think it does myself, but it's up to him.**

By the end of 1973, all the basic footage for the Zeppelin film was in the can. But a further three years would elapse before it finally reached the screen.

November 1973

The Zeppelin organisation had bought Headley Grange in Hampshire as a corporate headquarters, recording studio and rehearsal location, and the group were there continuing early work on the next album.
    At the same time, Jimmy Page was finishing work on the soundtrack for 'Lucifer Rising', a film by Kenneth Anger, an author, ex-actor and film-maker who shared Page's interest in the occult and was also a disciple of Aleister Crowley.

Jimmy Page: **I've always got on very well with Anger. He's a good friend, really. He's never been as awe-inspiring and unapproachable to me as some would probably tell you. It's just . . . one day he asked me to toss some ideas around for a soundtrack and I went away feeling something but never being able to really express it, until one day when it all sort of poured out and I got down immediately to recording it.**

December 1973

12

John Paul Jones appears on the TV show 'Colour My Soul' with Madeleine Bell.

Jones had helped write and produce Ms. Bell's 'Comin' Atcha' album over the preceding months, as well as playing on Jobriath's 'Creatures Of The Streets'.

1974

January 1974

At a London press conference, Peter Grant and Atlantic chief Ahmet Ertegun announced the formation of Led Zeppelin's own label, to be distributed by Atlantic.

As Zeppelin's original contract had expired before Christmas, this move was no surprise and they were by no means the first big band to acquire their own record company. But, unlike most of the others, Zeppelin fully intended that theirs would be a proper label, with a roster of acts, rather than just a vehicle for their own output.

Robert Plant: **The people involved with us who will be on the label – Maggie Bell, The Pretty Things, Bad Company (except Paul Rodgers who was big before with Free) were all with record companies that didn't do very much for them. We're going to try and pull it off for them, and that's what this record company means to me.**

Atlantic Spokesperson: **It's a good investment, both in terms of money and artistic satisfaction. They wanted to build something of lasting financial value. And they can also help the music of others be heard.**

February 1974

14

Page, Plant and Bonham join old friend and new signee Roy Harper for his St. Valentine's Day concert at London's Rainbow Theatre. Plant compères the evening, almost unrecognisable in leopard skin drapes and duck-tailed hair-do.

Meanwhile, recording for the sixth Zeppelin album continued slowly but surely.

Robert Plant: **In three weeks we managed to spend at least three days a week recording . . . between various calamities, the Roy Harper gig we did at the Rainbow Theatre on Valentine's Day, highs and lows and all. And we got eight tracks off. A lot of them are really raunchy . . . real belters with live vocals. I'm really pleased with them.**

You have to understand that we can never plan out an album. Some musicians are capable of

March 1974

During recording sessions, a name for Zeppelin's hitherto anonymous label was found.

Jimmy Page: **I had a long acoustic guitar instrumental with just sparse vocal sections – the song was about twenty minutes long and the vocal was about six minutes, and the whole thing was quite epic really. Almost semi-classical, I suppose, and I had bits of it and we were recording with the truck and there was no title**

sitting down methodically, but we're not like that. Our music is an excitement thing. It can be impromptu. It drops out of your mind, falls out of your head on to the floor and you pick it up as it bounces. That's how we work. But what can you expect? We hire a recording truck and trudge off to some shitty old house in the country. The last thing you'd expect is for the music to fall right into place. We even spent one night down there sitting around drinking ourselves under the table and telling each other how good we were. It was a good time

and the album has some real belters.

for it, and someone shouted out 'What's it going to be called?' and I shouted out 'Swan Song!', and the whole thing stopped and we said what a great name for the LP. All the vibes started and suddenly it was out of the LP and on to the record label. I think Swan Song is a good name for a record label, because if you don't have success on Swan Song . . . well then, you shouldn't have signed up with them.

As well as investing in Swan Song, Zeppelin were helping to finance the film 'Monty Python and The Holy Grail', together with Pink Floyd and Charisma Records.

April 1974

Swansong acquired office premises in London's Kings Road and in the Manhattan area of New York.

Jimmy Page was also in the property market on his own behalf, outbidding David Bowie to buy actor Richard Harris's house in Kensington for a modest £350,000.

Personally, however, the group were keeping a very low profile, giving the odd interview but otherwise keeping themselves to themselves.

Robert Plant: **I could have the press come up and watch me milk my goats and all that stuff, but what we really have to give out to audiences is our music, and much of that comes from travelling and from the privacy we have in our home life.**

May 1974

The Swansong label was launched in America with two parties, one at the Four Seasons restaurant in New York (which set the new label back $10,000), and the other at the Bel Air Hotel in Los Angeles, with over 150 guests, including Groucho Marx, ex-Monkee Micky Dolenz and Bill Wyman.

In the evening after the New York luncheon, the group went to see Mott The Hoople at the Uris Theatre on Broadway, and got into some disagreements backstage when Mott declined Bonham's offer to jam with them.

25

'Melody Maker' announce that Zeppelin will be playing at an open-air festival to be held at Knebworth, in Hertfordshire. This announcement turns out to be premature (five years premature, to be exact).

Robert Plant: **I won't deny that there had been talks about a possibility of us appearing, but there were a few things that weren't just right, and therefore absolutely nothing was confirmed. Unfortunately, it seems that Freddie Bannister (the promoter) jumped the gun on that one, which is a pity because we've worked well together in the past. Obviously, we're really sorry that this happened and that the press got hold of the story, because it must look like we're going back on our word. If we had, then someone should be sueing us.**

July 1974

The new album was now in the remixing stages, although its actual release was still several months away.

Robert Plant: **On the surface, this band might not appear to be a hive of industry, but when we do get something together, it's always something that we're all**

completely satisfied with. That's the reason we never ever rush things or try to push our luck.

You owe it to every single member in a group to take things at a communal, even pace and then, when you do get together, you're really keen to work hard. Some of the tracks we've recorded for this new album are superb, and they were created in the old-fashioned way of just running through one track . . . and before we even knew where we were, we'd have something totally different happening.

August 1974

John Paul Jones joined Dave Gilmour from Pink Floyd and

Steve Broughton from The Edgar Broughton Band to back Roy Harper at an open-air free concert in Hyde Park.

In an interview with 'Melody Maker', Page admitted that the album would not be out in September as originally planned. This was partly due to the fact that work on the film had held up work on the record.

By then, Joe Massot, who had directed nearly all the basic footage for the movie, had been replaced because "he's got the priorities a bit mixed up, and he missed a lot of stuff as well." The new man in charge was Peter Clifton, an Australian whose credentials included work on films with Hendrix, The Stones and Chuck Berry.

September 1974

14

All the members of Zeppelin attend the mammoth Crosby,

Stills, Nash & Young concert at Wembley Stadium.

Later in the month, Page was in the States to jam with Bad Company at gigs in New York's Central Park and Austin, Texas. Swansong's first signings were in the middle of an incredibly successful American début which established them instantly as one of the biggest bands in rock.

At home, John Paul Jones did his bit to keep the property market buoyant, putting his house at Cranborough, Sussex, up for sale at £97,500.

October 1974

Bad Company's first album got Swansong off to the best possible start when it topped the US charts towards the end of their Stateside tour.

31

To celebrate the first Swansong release in UK, 'Silk Torpedo' by The Pretty Things, Zeppelin throw a Hallowe'en party at Chislehurst Caves.

Melody Maker: **The cost of the event was comparable to a sizeable deposit on a country mansion, a spokesman claimed later. Certainly no expense was spared**

in the name of entertainment.

Naked or half-naked women lined the various dark recesses of the caves, or reclined before sacrificial altars. There were fire eaters, illusionists, enough booze to keep a small off-licence reasonably well stocked for a month (all of which was duly consumed).

November 1974

26

Rehearsals for the forthcoming North American tour, set to begin after the New Year, begin at Liveware, a converted theatre in Ealing.

Jimmy Page: **At the moment I've got to start building up my stamina, because every time I've toured the States I've returned a physical . . . and mental wreck. I mean, after the last tour they tried to get me put in a mental hospital. It was either that or going to a monastery! Ultimately, I just went to sleep for a month.**

This time, I'm definitely going to take a 'juicer' along with me. I mean, I used to be a vegetarian and *that* was like committing suicide in America. The last time I ended up just eating hamburgers and at the end I was just a complete mess. This time though – precautions are going to be taken.

December 1974

16

Jimmy Page and John Paul Jones take a break from Zeppelin rehearsals to join Bad Company on stage at the Rainbow.

Jimmy Page: **1974 didn't really happen. 1975 will be a better year.**

1975

January 1975

11
Rotterdam.

12
Brussels.

The first Zeppelin gigs for 18 months were low-key affairs, designed as warm-ups for the monster American excursion ahead. Backstage at the Brussels date, Robert Plant was interviewed by Bob Harris for the 'Old Grey Whistle Test'. The programme featuring the interview was transmitted five days later.

Back in London, the Page pinkies were in bother again. The guitarist broke the ring finger of his left hand in a train door at Victoria station. Fortunately the tour was able to go ahead as planned, although 'Dazed and Confused' (traditionally an excuse for guitar wizardry during Zeppelin's performances) had to be left out on the earlier dates.

Further bad news came across the Atlantic, where the group were banned from appearing in Boston after rioting in ticket queues had occurred at the Boston Garden. This was particularly sad, as Boston had been one of the first cities to take Zeppelin to its heart, and held a special place in their affections.

The planned tour was slightly shorter than its predecessor in terms of towns visited (26 as opposed to 33), but in other respects its scale was every bit as monolithic.

Financial details were not given, perhaps because of the criticism such bragging had attracted in the

past. But the 700,000 tickets were all sold before the first night. The 44-man tour party was the largest yet, as were the 70,000 watt PA system and 310,000 watt lighting rig. They'd also added some new effects since the last time, including the use of lasers.

Another improvement was that, while still using the Starship to ferry them from gig to gig, the group were basing themselves in single hotels for whole sections of the tour, to cut down on the constant changes of environment which are usually such a drawback of life on the road. For the first few dates, they were staying at the Ambassador Hotel in Chicago, then they moved on to the New York Plaza, and for the West Coast section of the tour, they put up at the Hyatt House in Hollywood.

18
The 10th American tour opens in Minneapolis.

20, 21, 22
Chicago Stadium. During these concerts, Plant was suffering from flu. He struggled on through gigs in Cleveland and Indianapolis, but the St. Louis concert, scheduled for the 27th, had to be postponed until mid-February.

While Plant recovered in Chicago, the rest of the band popped off for a couple of days in Los Angeles.

29
Greensboro, North Carolina. The first date after the unplanned hiatus, marked by rioting between police and fans without tickets.

Melody Maker: **Although the majority of the rioting fans had disappeared by the end of the**

show, the group were forced to make the quickest getaway within seconds after leaving the stage. Zeppelin manager Peter Grant took the wheel of one of the limousines – much to the surprise of the official driver – while the other was driven by Magnet, a British roadie employed by Deep Purple, who had come along to the concert as an old friend of the band.

Heading the procession was a police car which cleared the way for the two limousines, sirens blasting at speeds of up to 70mph in a heavily built-up area. The three cars drove over red lights and on the opposite side of the road in a scene that resembled a Steve McQueen movie car chase. The squealing tyres almost drowned out the police siren.

Grant, an expert driver, who had offered to buy both limousines from the car company, said afterwards 'I didn't care what happened so long as I got the boys out OK. That car I was driving was out of tune, otherwise I'd have driven faster still'.

To everyone's relief, the next few dates in Montreal, Detroit and Pittsburgh were rather more conventional affairs.

February 1975

3
New York, Madison Square Garden.

4
Long Island, Nassau Colosseum.

7
Madison Square Garden.

10
Washington.

Zeppelin were even bigger than before, and indisputably the top act in the business.

Robert Plant: **It's not just that we think we're the best group in the world. It's just that we think we're so much better than whoever is Number Two.**

'Black Country Woman' and 'The Rover' were originally intended for 'Houses Of The Holy'.

Jimmy Page: **As usual, we had more material than the required 40-odd minutes for one album. We had enough material for one and a half LPs, so we figured let's put out a double and use some of the material we had done previously but never released. It seemed like a good time to do that sort of thing, release tracks like 'Boogie With Stu', which we wouldn't normally be able to do.**

For once, Led Zeppelin got an almost unanimous thumbs-up from reviewers, and the album shot to the top of charts around the world in record time. In America, it

also pulled the rest of the Zeppelin catalogue along with it, and they became the first rock band ever to have six albums on the Billboard Top 200 simultaneously. It hardly seemed possible, but by the end of that tenth American tour, Led

12
Madison Square Garden.

13, 14
Nassau Colosseum. Originally, only two nights at the Colosseum were planned, but a third night was arranged to accommodate Zeppelin fans who had been disappointed by the Boston cancellation.

As always, the New York stay was one of the tour's social, as well as musical highpoints. Mick Jagger and David Bowie were at the Garden, Ron Wood and Rod Stewart at Nassau, and a string of parties kept the band occupied during off-stage hours. However, the legendary Zeppelin road fever (restructuring hotels, groupies unlimited, etc.) was apparently less in evidence on this tour. Possibly because Page, with his damaged hand, Plant with his lingering flu bug, and Bonham with stomach trouble, were all feeling in less than peak condition.

March 1975

After a ten-day break, the second half of the tour ran through Texas (where Bonham added a custom Corvette to his car collection) to the West Coast of Canada and the States (where he added to it further, with a Ford hot rod which he took dragging on Sunset Strip).

24, 25, 27
The tour ends with three dates at the L.A. Forum.

Robert Plant: **Looking back on it, this tour's been a flash. Really fast. Very poetic too. Lots of battles and conquests, backdropped by the din of the hordes. Aside from the fact that it's been our most successful tour on every level, I just found myself having a great time all the way through.**
We had no trouble adjusting to the tour at all. Normally it takes a while to get into the swing of things. Not this time. I've never been more into a tour before. The music's jelled amazingly well. Everyone loved 'Physical Graffiti'. That meant a lot. It's like we're on an incredible winning streak.

The band had been previewing several songs from the new album on stage, and by the time it was released in early March, advance orders in the USA exceeded a million copies.
Zeppelin's first double set, 'Physical Graffiti' included several tunes from earlier album sessions, as well as the fruits of the previous year's recording. 'Bron-y-Aur' was from the 'Led Zeppelin III' sessions; 'Down By The Seaside', 'Night Flight' and 'Boogie With Stu' from the fourth album; and

April 1975

19
Tickets go on sale for three concerts at Earls Court in May, Led Zeppelin's first British dates since January 1973. All 51,000 go within two hours. Another two nights are hastily added, and the further 34,000 tickets are snapped up over a weekend.

May 1975

The Earls Court concerts were regarded as something of a milestone, by both the band and the media. The size of the venue meant that Zeppelin were at last able to use their full American stage production, plus video screens, in front of a British audience. They rehearsed for three days before the concerts began, to iron out any equipment problems and to blow away the cobwebs after their six-week layoff since the American tour.

LED ZEPPELIN

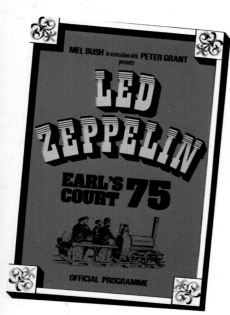

MEL BUSH in association with PETER GRANT presents

LED ZEPPELIN
EARL'S COURT '75

OFFICIAL PROGRAMME

In the press excitement built up, with every music paper running a special feature on the group. Even 'The Observer' devoted eight pages to documenting their achievements.

17, 18, 23, 24, 25
Earls Court concerts. Zeppelin's sets last between three and four hours every night, and include an acoustic section.

Ian Knight (Showco stage director): **When you look at the size of a hall like this, people automatically believe Led Zeppelin are going to earn a fortune from these shows. Well, they're not. Not when you compare the sheer expense of staging such an event in ratio to the low ticket prices. I can tell you,**

Zeppelin can consider themselves lucky if they break even.

I know it must sound ludicrous for me to be standing here telling you that a band can play to 17,000 people for five nights and still not make money, but the overheads are so incredibly high and the only way Zeppelin could show a healthy profit from this would be to charge £5 to £6 a ticket. But that's not what they're into.

John Bonham: **I thought they were the best shows that we've ever put on in England. I always get tense before a show, and we were expecting trouble from such a huge audience.**

But everything went really well, and although we couldn't have the laser beams at full power, I thought the video screen was well worth doing. It cost a lot of bread, but you could see close-

ups you'd never be able to see normally at a concert. It was worth every penny.

June 1975

Good news and bad news for John Bonham at the start of the month. His wife Pat gave birth to a daughter, Zoe, and he was banned from driving for six months.

In fact, this latter inconvenience was of little importance, since Bonham and the rest of the band were about to leave Britain for an indefinite period of holidays/tax exile. Plant's dedication of 'In My Time Of Dying' to Chancellor Denis Healey at Earls Court took on a new significance as Zeppelin set up temporary HQ at Montreux, in order to avoid handing most of their hard-earned lucre straight over to HM Government.

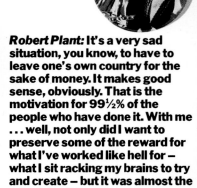

Robert Plant: **It's a very sad situation, you know, to have to leave one's own country for the sake of money. It makes good sense, obviously. That is the motivation for 99½% of the people who have done it. With me . . . well, not only did I want to preserve some of the reward for what I've worked like hell for – what I sit racking my brains to try and create – but it was almost the principle of the thing.**

Plant had left England immediately after the Earls Court dates for a family holiday in Morocco, and three weeks later he met up with Jimmy Page in Marrakesh. From there, the two of them embarked on a long journey through the Sahara by Range Rover.

Robert Plant: **Once you get off the normal tourist path and have the right vehicle, so long as you know a little bit of Arabic, which I do, then you discover they are quite fine people. They're very warm people, and they're overjoyed when they find you have taken the trouble to learn their language.**

We tried to get down as far as the Spanish Sahara at the time when the war was just breaking out. There was a distinct possibility that we could have got very, very lost, going round in circles and taking ages to get out. It's such a vast country with no landmarks and no people apart from the odd tent and a camel.

We kept reaching these army road blocks where we'd get machine guns pointed at us and we'd have to wave our passports furiously and say we were going to bathe at the next beach. Then we'd go on 30 miles to another road block and claim we were only going along to the next beach again. We got as far as we could, but eventually the road got so bad, we had to turn back.

July 1975

From Morocco, Page and Plant travelled up through Spain and France to Montreux, where they met Grant, Bonham and Jones for a prearranged group meeting. Here they were given details of their next American schedule, another 33-date marathon starting on August 23rd, with the possibility of Zeppelin's first South American

dates being added at the end.

The group stayed in Montreux to attend the annual jazz festival, run by Zeppelin's old friend Claude Nobs, before going their separate ways again. Page and Plant set off together with their families, heading for the Greek island of Rhodes to enjoy their last few days of leisure in the sun.

August 1975

3

Jimmy Page leaves Rhodes to go to Italy, arranging to meet up with Plant and the rest of Zeppelin in Paris five days later, to begin rehearsals for the tour.

4

The hired car in which Plant and his family are travelling hits a tree. His wife Maureen suffers a fractured pelvis and skull, the children (who are sitting in the back seat) escape with minor injuries, and Plant himself has multiple fractures of the ankle and elbow.

***Robert Plant:* After the crash, I looked across at Maureen and thought she had stopped breathing. She was in a terrible state. We didn't have an ambulance to take us to hospital. We were put in an open fruit truck. It was so low that my leg trailed on the ground.**

Initially, the family were cared for at a local hospital, but as soon as possible they were airlifted back to London.

***Robert Plant:* If we hadn't had the money available to fly to England right away for the best medical treatment, I'm certain my wife wouldn't be alive now.**

Maureen would have to spend several weeks in hospital, and the diagnosis was almost as bad for Plant. Doctors told him he wouldn't walk again for at least six months, so all the group's plans to fill their year of tax exile with a round-the-world tour had to be cancelled.

The accident had come at the worst possible time, as Plant discovered almost as soon as he'd got settled in London.

***New Musical Express:* In somewhat less than sedate circum-**

stances, an imperilled Robert Plant barely avoided the sweaty grip of the taxman over the weekend.

The Zep vocalist, heavily doused in plaster casts, was forced to flee the country when it was discovered that his "tax exile period" was rapidly drawing to a close . . . that another day in Britain would render him liable to a full year's tax whack.

Having airlifted himself and wife Maureen from Rhodes back to London at a cost of £7,000, Plant was having no more serious assaults on his wallet.

So . . . multiple fractures and all, he had himself installed on to a waiting plane at London's Heathrow airport and buzzed to the Channel Island of Jersey – marginally outside the tax net of that Man from the Treasury.

According to reports he was so extensively covered in plaster that he had to be hoisted aboard by a fork-lift truck!

In true showbiz manner Plant made his deadline with nary six hours to spare.

Shortly afterwards, there were reports that John Paul Jones was also in the wars, having broken his hand.

September 1975

In one sense, Jersey was the perfect place for Plant to be, since he could be visited easily by London specialists without being bothered by the taxman. But for a lad used to a modicum of excitement, it was a trifle quiet, so as soon as his injuries were healing satisfactorily, he was moved to Los Angeles, and from there to a beach house at Malibu.

***Robert Plant:* Being out on the beach was a blessing and a great stimulation for me. Then, in late summer, a freak storm developed and they were having trouble keeping Malibu intact. I'd wake up in the morning and go to my little spot on the beach where I**

watched the sandpipers, and find that ten feet of beach had disappeared overnight. I kept looking at the little wooden house I was living in and saying to myself 'That's all I need now — to have that drop on me foot or me head'.

But I said to myself, 'We have all this time now, why don't we use it and make an album?'

Accordingly, Jimmy Page joined Plant in Malibu and together they began working on new material, much of it inspired by Plant's frame of mind following the trauma of the accident.

On a brighter note, 'Melody Maker' readers had once again done Led Zeppelin proud in their annual poll. In the British section, the group picked up awards for Top Male Singer, Top Album, Top Group and Best Live Act, while in the International section they won the Male Singer, Guitarist and Album categories. Jimmy Page and John Bonham went to the awards ceremony at the Carlton Tower later in the month to pick up their prizes.

October 1975

From Malibu, the call went out to John Bonham and John Paul Jones that their services were now required, and the whole group convened in Los Angeles.

Robert Plant: In L.A. we just rehearsed and rehearsed. It was so strange for me the first time, because I was sitting in an armchair singing, and I found myself wiggling inside my cast. The whole band really wanted to play and had wanted to do that tour, so the same effort was put into the album. It was a unique situation where we rehearsed for three weeks — on and off in true Zeppelin style because we're not the greatest band for rehearsing. We've always felt that too much rehearsing on a song can spoil it for us . . . sort of take the edge off the excitement. But this time it worked in the opposite way, because the enthusiasm was contained in such a small space of time.

November 1975

With rehearsals concluded, the scene shifted to Musicland Studios in Munich, where the group had booked a month's studio time. One Zeppelin member (who remained nameless) turned up late, however, and they were left with less than three weeks. Under normal circumstances, that would have been just about enough time to record one track, but the group's frustration at their enforced absence from home and their inability to play live was channelled into a burst of energy that saw the album completely finished, including remixing, in just 18 days.

Robert Plant: **I think we only went out twice. We were really too tired to do anything but put our heads down. It was like 14 hours a night, 18 days.**

The only bad moment came when Robert Plant almost undid the months of healing on his injured ankle in one mad moment.

Robert Plant: **I was hobbling around in the middle of this great track when suddenly my enthusiasm got the better of me. I was running to the vocal booth with this orthopaedic crutch when down I went, straight down on the bad foot. There was an almighty crack and a great flash of light and pain and I folded up in agony.**

I've never known Jimmy move so quickly. He was out of the mixing booth and holding me up, fragile as he might be, within a second. He became quite Germanic in his organisation of things and instantly I was rushed off to hospital again in case I'd reopened the fracture, and if I had I would never have walked properly again.

December 1975

After completing the album, the group went back to Jersey to continue their tax exile as close to home as possible.

10
The members of Led Zeppelin make an unexpected appearance at Behan's nightclub, backing resident pianist Norman Hale, who had once played with The Tornadoes.

Robert Plant: **You see the possibility of playing and who can avoid it, you know? It was like rock 'n' roll night at this dance hall that was like some place ten years gone by, in the best old English tradition.**
  Guys with dicky bows and evening jackets ready to bang your head against a wall if you stepped out of line, and chairs and tables lined up in escalation. Chicks wearing suspenders and stockings and a lot of rock 'n' roll.
  Bonzo said 'C'mon man, let's plan on going'. And I said 'Look, man, I can't even walk for God's sake, don't embarrass me. I can't hobble across the dance floor and on to the stage'. He said we'd go through the side door and then up the back steps. And with amazing grace, that's what I did and I found myself plonked on a stool. But I really was shy.

Every time I went to hit a note, I stood up. Not putting any weight on my foot, but just sort of standing. Oh, there were some great photos.
  Of course, I made sure that I sat almost behind Bonzo, wedged between the drums and the piano . . . but then I found myself edging forward just a little bit. Then, after the third number, I was wiggling the stool past the drums and further out, you know. And it was like another flash of white light. It was great, really good. Except for we wouldn't stop playing. They kept flashing the lights inside the place and really like 'Get them off the stage now, they've done enough'.

24
John Bonham, John Paul Jones and Robert Plant return home to spend Christmas with their families, while Jimmy Page flies to New York to mix the soundtrack for the film.

31
Robert Plant walks unaided for the first time since the accident.

1976

January 1976

Having used up most of the precious days they were allowed at home during their "non-resident" tax year, Plant, Bonham and Jones joined Page in New York. From their base at the Park Lane Hotel, they gave some press interviews and spent a fairly hectic social month, while Page continued work on the film soundtrack.

Robert Plant was walking again by now, but the interviews left no doubt that relief at the speed of his recovery was severely offset by the misery of the group's involuntary nomadic lifestyle.

Robert Plant: **We all want to go home ... It's a very personal thing whether you want to go or stay, and it aggravates me that people have worked for something for a long time and they've had to leave because of these tax laws. New York, grey as it may be, is full of some of the finest English talent, not just music but sports personalities and actors, and anybody who has a flair for something.**

My reward for all the things I've done should be to be able to go back and be with Maureen and the children. The situation in England is terrible for the creative output that musicians are capable of. It's bad for England – period.

It's a very pitiful situation when a lot of the more established musicians have to flee. You only have to go from here and four skyscrapers down the street there's Mick Jagger. He'd echo the same thing. We're all holed up in little boxes here looking over Central Park. It's very, very sad.

February 1976

11

The 'New Musical Express' Readers Poll appears, with Zeppelin very nearly sweeping the board: Top British Male Vocalist, Top British Group, Top International Male Vocalist, Top International Group, Top Guitarist, Top Producer, Best Album and Best Dressed Album.

Earlier, the press had reported that the forthcoming album would be called 'Obelisk', relating to the 2001-type object featured prominently on the cover. The cover wouldn't change, but the title would.

Jimmy Page: **The way the cover came about was that after we'd returned from the recording, we realised that the only feasible** thing to do was to take a picture of the studio and its chaos, but we needed something better than that, so we contacted Hipgnosis and explained to the chap there, Po, what had been going on.

He returned and said that the thing that had always struck him about Led Zeppelin was a power, a force, an alchemical quality which was indefinable, which I guess he was relating to the magnitude of the band. He came up with this idea of interpreting this through an object which could be related to any object in a community that everyone was perfectly at home with.

March 1976

Leaving the rest of the group in America, Jimmy Page returned to the UK to give some press interviews prior to the release of the new album, which was now officially entitled 'Presence'.

Jimmy Page: **It was recorded while the group was on the move, technological gypsies. No base, no home. All you could relate to was a new horizon and a suitcase. So there's a lot of movement and aggression. A lot of bad feeling towards being put in that situation.**

Also, we're playing more as a band than on any LP before. Everybody's playing in such a way as to bring out everybody else. I'm really happy with it, and

I'm not usually that optimistic about them because I've lived every mistake over and over.

There's so many things that have come out from those conditions of having to finish it in a certain time. I was amazed at the inventiveness, the fact that no overdubs were wasted ... Just totally taking chances, experimentation, and they seemed to work.

Dave Dee (Atlantic executive): **This Zeppelin album is going to be a monster. It will be the biggest Zeppelin album in this country ever. We were prepared for this one. We heard the tapes of the album some time ago and knew demand would be enormous. Everyone here is very enthusiastic about it.**

April 1976

When 'Presence' became available for public consumption, after yet another lengthy delay over artwork, it met with a mixed reaction, like nearly all the earlier Zeppelin albums.

Chris Welch (Melody Maker): **The combination of studio, producer, compositions and energy on the session has worked with that indefinable chemistry that everybody hopes will result when it comes to making an album.**

This single album has certainly caught Zeppelin with their atomic particles flying, if you will pardon the expression.

Charles Shaar Murray (New Musical Express): **I thought my razor was dull until I heard this album ... despite the excellence of the playing, singing and production, 'Presence' never gets any higher than simply being a demonstration of capabilities and an exercise in style.**

In the UK, despite moving swiftly to the Number One spot, 'Presence' didn't quite live up to

Dave Dee's optimistic forecasts. But in the USA it was the first album ever to go platinum on advance orders alone.

May 1976

23

Jimmy Page and Robert Plant attend Bad Company's concert at the L.A. Forum, and join them on-stage for an ad hoc set of standards.

26

The members of Led Zeppelin return to the UK.

27

John Paul Jones jams with The Pretty Things at the Marquee.

July 1976

Jimmy Page and John Bonham went to studios in Switzerland to work on an all-percussion track of Bonham's own devising, which was intended for the next Zeppelin studio album but has yet to see the light of day.

On returning to England, Page found himself on the receiving end of a crude attack by Kenneth Anger in an interview with 'Sounds'. Anger claimed that Page had failed to deliver the soundtrack for 'Lucifer Rising', and made several other wild allegations.

Jimmy Page: **I not only delivered the music but I lent him the machinery we'd had for work on our movie, 'The Song Remains The Same'. He hadn't got the money to hire the stuff, so I let him have all our editing machinery and everything so he could finish his film.**

In fact, if you read between the lines, it'll be apparent that maybe the creditors were on his back for

him to deliver the finished film and because he hadn't got it he used me as a scapegoat and an excuse . . .

Now whether he thought in his mind that he was indebted to me somehow and that he felt he had to get me off his back, I don't know. I mean, I didn't start hassling. I just wanted to see the bloke finish the bloody film. I mean its whole history is so absurd, anyway. I just assumed that it was unfinished because he was such a perfectionist and he'd always end up going over his budgets. All I can say is: Anger's time was all that was needed to finish that film. Nothing else!

Talking of films, 'The Song Remains The Same' was now completed, at last, and set for release before the end of the year.

October 1976

18

The double album soundtrack of 'The Song Remains The Same' is released.

20

World première of 'The Song Remains The Same' at New York's Cinema One. It is a charity première, raising over $25,000 for the Save The Children Fund, and is followed by a party at the Pierre Hotel. A few days later the West Coast première is held in Los Angeles.

Jimmy Page: **They held them apart by a few days so we could check the cinemas out. It's not as easy a job as you'd think getting the sound right for cinemas. I remember seeing 'Woodstock' and they had towers of speakers.**

Well, the first time in New York was great, the first time one had sat in an audience. Every time I had seen the film before was with technicians, people with a really critical eye. Then the film really lived for the first time and you could see people getting off on things, applauding and laughing at the right time, generally vibing.

23

Led Zeppelin's first-ever appearance on American TV, playing 'Black Dog' and an edited 'Dazed and Confused' on Don Kirshner's Rock Concert Show.

November 1976

2

BBC's 'Old Grey Whistle Test' shows an interview with Robert Plant and Peter Grant, conducted a few days earlier aboard a boat on the Thames.

4

The UK première of 'The Song Remains The Same' takes place simultaneously at the Warner West End and ABC, Shaftesbury Avenue cinemas.

The movie won some acclaim in film circles, picking up awards from 'Films & Filming' magazine for the Best Documentary and Best Soundtrack of the year, but music critics were largely hostile. Sometimes extremely so.

Robert Duncan (Circus): **The Zep movie is sort of what would have happened if 'Help!' had taken itself seriously as film noire. And been written and produced, directed and edited by junior college students who had just discovered LSD.**

Dave Marsh (Rolling Stone): It is hard to imagine any other major rock act making a film so guileless and revealing. Far from a monument to Zeppelin's stardom, 'The Song Remains The Same' is a tribute to their rapaciousness and inconsideration. While Led Zeppelin's music remains worthy of respect (even if their best songs are behind them) their sense of themselves merits only contempt.

Chris Charlesworth (Melody Maker): It has been three years in the making, but 'The Song Remains The Same' is a classy, and surely enormously successful, film.

Successful it certainly was, especially across the Atlantic, where the film grossed over $200,000 in its first week and the soundtrack album went platinum in advance. But perhaps the most pertinent comment on its actual merits was Peter Grant's reference to it as "the most expensive home movie ever made".

With the brouhaha surrounding the film launch out of the way, and Robert Plant fully fit again, the group were able to get down to rehearsing for the American tour set to start in February.

December 1976

Rehearsals continued right through the month.

Jimmy Page: So much of this year has been taken up with petty little time-consuming things. It's not been a static period so much as an unsatisfying one. There have been so many niggling little things to take care of – things so petty that readers would never believe Jimmy Page rock guitarist would need to involve himself with.

It's changing now, though. I mean, playing live – that whole stimulus – has been missing, and Christ, when we did that first rehearsal it just clicked all over again. I just feel that I've cleaned out a load of problems and now I'm ready to get back in the fray, so to speak.

Something epic is going to happen musically anyway. That's what I feel. This next tour . . . you'll see.

1977

January 1977

As the tour dates loomed nearer, rehearsals moved to the more spacious surroundings of Manticore, ELP's converted cinema in Fulham. There they were visited by 'New Musical Express', in the wake of yet another string of victories in that paper's Readers Poll.

Jimmy Page: I think that if you've got a set that's so cut and dried, so well-rehearsed that you've no other option but to play it note-for-note each night, then it's bound to get stagnant.

We've always structured things so there's an element in which we can suddenly shoot off on something entirely different and see what's happening. Personally speaking, for me, that's where the element of change and surprise comes in – the possibilities of having that kind of freedom, should you suddenly require it, right in the middle of a number.

20

Jimmy Page and Robert Plant take time off from rehearsing to see The Damned at the Roxy, in London's Covent Garden. The Roxy is the country's major punk venue, and the pair are the first (indeed the only) prominent members of the "old guard" to venture into it.

24

Plant goes there again, this time accompanied by John Bonham.

Robert Plant: You ask me if it reminds me of when we were

starting out, but it doesn't. It reminds me of when we were rehearsing this afternoon! There's that same *feel* for the music . . . and all the talk about Old Farts and Young Farts is nonsense, age doesn't matter.

February 1977

Disaster once again. Only days before Zeppelin were due to fly out to start the American tour, Robert Plant went down with tonsillitis and the whole thing had to be postponed for over a month.

This was doubly inconvenient, since all the group's gear had already been shipped across to the States, so for the next few weeks they were unable to keep in trim . . . why they didn't just go out and buy some more equipment has never been explained.

April 1977

1

The eleventh US tour opens at the Dallas Memorial Auditorium.

This was to be Zeppelin's biggest tour ever, 51 dates in 30 cities, running through until mid-August with a couple of two-week breaks in between, and taking them in front of over 1,300,000 fans.

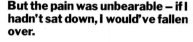

Following on from their last gigs, at Earls Court way back in May '75, the performances were featuring an acoustic set and the use of video screens in larger venues. Performances were once again running over three hours, with a basic 15-song selection from the Zeppelin catalogue followed by encores of 'Whole Lotta Love' and 'Rock 'n' Roll'.

As on previous American tours, the group were based at hotels in Chicago, New York and Los Angeles, and commuting on board the Starship.

3

Oklahoma City, Myriad.

6–10

Chicago Stadium. One of the four nights in the Windy City is marred when the set has to be stopped after only an hour, because Jimmy Page is ill.

Jimmy Page: **They think it was food poisoning. It's the first time we've ever stopped a gig like that. We always have a go, really, because we're not a rip-off band.**

But the pain was unbearable – if I hadn't sat down, I would've fallen over.

12, 13

Minneapolis and St. Paul.

15

St. Louis, Blues Arena.

17

Indianapolis, Market Square Arena.

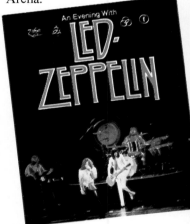

19, 20

Cincinatti, Riverfront Coliseum. The first night here is the scene of a hundred arrests, as 1000 ticketless fans try to gatecrash the hall.

23

Atlanta.

25

Louisville.

27, 28

Cleveland, Richfield Coliseum.

One of the Cleveland performances was pirated as the album 'Destroyer'. Bootlegging was a problem that dogged Zeppelin throughout their career, even though Peter Grant was always most zealous in his efforts to prevent recording equipment of any kind being brought into

Zeppelin concerts.

In fact, at one stage, he had been unable to enter Canada for a year after bopping a gentleman with a machine at a Vancouver show. He turned out to be an employee of the government monitoring noise levels.

30

Pontiac Silverdome. 76,229 people attend this gig, the largest ever audience for a single rock band, paying nearly $800,000 between them.

May 1977

The first two weeks of the month were holiday time, as Jimmy Page headed for Cairo and the rest of the band for home.

Jimmy Page: **I was going to go to Cairo on the tour break and I was tossing up whether to go or not. And there was this TV programme hosted by Omar Sharif about the mysteries of the Pyramids. And they showed this old footage of the Pyramids with a Zeppelin flying in and I thought 'That's it, I'll definitely go'. It seemed to be such a strange coincidence that that bit of footage should be there on the day I was thinking about it.**

Certificates:— Guy Woolfenden
Trevor Nunn

SPECIAL AWARDS

Statuettes:— Led Zeppelin *for their contribution to British music*

12
The members of Zeppelin and Peter Grant go to London's Grosvenor House to receive an Ivor Novello Award for their "colourful and energetic contribution to British music".

18
Birmingham Coliseum, Alabama.

19
Baton Rouge.

21
Houston, The Summit.

22
Houston, Convention Centre.

25–30
Largo, Capitol Centre.

June 1977

3
Tampa Stadium. This concert has to be cancelled after 20 minutes, when rain starts getting on to the stage and threatening electrocution. Originally, a replacement date is intended, but the local authorities ban Zeppelin from returning after some of the 70,000 disappointed fans cause a disturbance.

7–14
New York, Madison Square Garden for six nights.

Ray Coleman (Melody Maker): **They skilfully inflict a muzzy paralysis over their audience, and few of their tunes are memorable, and their music doesn't actually** move you in the way, say, Buddy Holly or Bruce Springsteen catch ahold of your spine.

But Zeppelin seem to be still peculiarly, sadistically right for the Seventies. It's a fair bet that every fan left those New York concerts high on the gripping theatre of their act, for they most certainly strike a chord among a million kids.

19
San Diego Sports Arena.

21–27
Los Angeles Forum. Six nights.

At the end of this second leg of the tour, everything pointed to the trip being the best yet. Peter Grant, affected by his recent divorce, was keeping a lower profile than usual, but the rest of the Zeppelin team seemed healthy, happy and delighted to be back in action. The only slight cloud on the horizon was that audiences were generally rowdier than on earlier visits.

Robert Plant: **We are used to them, but it can be crazy. A lot of times they break up our concen-**tration. I'm watching Jimmy, or the group's watching me for a cue and suddenly a frisbee sails out of the audience and none of us sees it. We've all been hit by these on stage, but the firecrackers are much worse. They scare the hell out of us.

July 1977

17
The final stretch of the tour begins at the Seattle Kingdome.

20
Tempe Activities Centre.

23, 24
Oakland Coliseum.

In the space of five days, what had apparently been a good humoured and highly successful tour came to a premature end amidst violence, acrimony and tragedy.

Backstage at the first Oakland date, Peter Grant, John Bonham and bodyguard John Bindon attacked one of promoter Bill Graham's security men, who had refused to give Grant's son a nameplate from Zeppelin's dressing-room caravan. The security man had to be taken to hospital for treatment after the beating.

. The next day's concert only went ahead after Graham had signed a letter of indemnification, which was not binding since Graham had no legal right to act on behalf of his security man. And on the 25th the

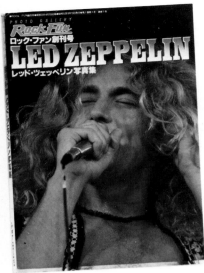

worth? It doesn't mean very much when you compare it to the love of a family.

August 1977

As the rest of the Zeppelin party made their melancholy way back to England, questions were already being raised about the future of the group. Rumours circulated that Robert Plant blamed Jimmy Page's occult interests for the appalling run of bad luck his family had suffered, and wanted no more to do with him.

three members of the Zeppelin entourage, along with tour manager Richard Cole who had allegedly assaulted another Graham employee, were arrested. All four men were charged with battery and freed on $250 bail. These criminal charges were shortly followed by a civil action, sueing the quartet for $2M damages.

The group left the Bay Area and this controversy behind them to visit New Orleans, the next stop along the way, but even worse news reached them there. On the 26th Robert Plant's five-year-old son Karac fell ill with a stomach infection. On the 27th his condition worsened so rapidly that an ambulance was called, but the boy was dead before reaching the hospital. Plant flew home immediately and the last seven dates were cancelled.

Robert Plant's Father: All this success and fame . . . what is it

Jimmy Page: All that was really tasteless. I think it was in really bad taste because, obviously, after the tragedy that Robert experienced, he needs time to be alone with his family . . .

. . . It's not karma at all. I don't see how the band would merit a karmic attack. All I or we have attempted to do is go out and really have a good time and please people at the same time. I always thought I was very fortunate through that, 'cause I can't think of anything better than doing what you really want to do and seeing just a mass of smiles. That's Utopia.

Everybody in this band is really determined to do the best for themselves and the people who've followed us up to now without bullshitting around. I just don't see how there could be bad karma or whatever.

I think it's just bad coincidence. OK, one may say there's no such thing as coincidence, but I really feel that.

September 1977

17

Jimmy Page plays a charity gig for Goaldiggers, a children's charity, at his 'local', the Half Moon in Plumpton. Jimmy joins Ron Wood and a Portsmouth band called Arms & Legs on stage, and the event raises £650.

Meanwhile, split rumours continued to circulate, and the idea that Zeppelin had some sort of hoo-doo on them was reinforced when John Bonham sustained two broken ribs in a car crash near his home.

October 1977

Jimmy Page eventually got so fed up with the supposition going on about Led Zeppelin's future, that he gave a string of interviews to all the major British music papers with the specific aim of denying any possibility of the band breaking up.

Jimmy Page: **Zeppelin's so close that no one person within the band would think twice about the situation. There is no question of splitting up. I know Robert wants to work again, and he'll start working at his own pace.**

In the same interviews, Page revealed that he had just had a new computer mixing facility installed at his home studio, and was keeping himself busy working on both new recordings and the assembling of a chronological live album, dating right back to the band's beginnings.

Jimmy Page: **I know there has been a live album, but I don't really consider it to be such, 'cos it was just a soundtrack, and by no means the best live stuff we have, but it had the celluloid. I've got tapes way back from the Albert Hall in 1969 and a couple from each year, so I'm slowly going through all of this picking out the gems.**

1978

February 1978

21

The criminal case against Peter Grant, John Bonham, Richard Cole and bodyguard John Bindon, arising from the incidents at Oakland Coliseum the previous July, is heard in California.

All four men, through their representatives, plead 'nolo contendere'. This means they are liable to conviction in the criminal case, without having to appear before judge and jury, but will still be able to deny charges in any civil action brought by Bill Graham's men. They each incur suspended prison sentences and fines ranging from $500 to $750.

Jack Berman (Zeppelin attorney): **Led Zeppelin has to be the happiest bunch of people on this earth right now.**

The judgement was indeed good news for the Zeppelin camp. Had the foursome been compelled to appear in the Californian court, they could have been presented with the civil lawsuits. As it was, Graham and his people would never succeed in getting them to court.

Bill Graham: **I can't believe that anyone can go into a trailer and kick the shit out of someone; and then the judge says 'Tut, tut, just be good boys from now on'. The real issue in the long run is that the only thing it cost them is something they have plenty of. So they'll never learn.**

They should have had to appear publicly to be charged, just like other mortals. What is learned here? That you cannot get away with this? . . . but you see, you can!

Money is not the issue, it never was. If they were made to walk into a court of law, then they'd know they aren't above the law. And next time they'd think of beating people up, it would act as a deterrent, but they didn't have to go through anything. They didn't have to give up anything that mattered to them. At worst, in the next couple of years they'll just be careful that they're not seen.

March 1978

Despite their lengthy silence, Led Zeppelin and the individual group members achieved an almost complete clean sweep of the awards in 'Creem' magazine's annual Readers Poll in America.

May 1978

Zeppelin started working as a group again with rehearsals at Clearwell Castle, in the Forest of Dean on the Welsh border. Shortly afterwards, 'Melody Maker' reported that these rehearsals heralded a new album and a possible tour, but this was not the case.

Jimmy Page: **That was basically a period of 'saying hello' to each other musically once again. We hadn't played together for so long, and Clearwell was the first actual playing we'd done for what seemed like an eternity, although it was only about 10 months. It was really just limbering up.**

July 1978

Robert Plant appeared in public for the first time since his son's death, sitting in with local bands around his Worcestershire home, including Melvin Giganticus and The Turd Burglars at Wolverly Memorial Hall.

August 1978

During a holiday on the Spanish island of Ibiza, Robert Plant appeared on stage at the Club Amnesia with R&B band Dr. Feelgood.

September 1978

15

Zeppelin tour manager Richard Cole gets married at Chelsea Register Office, and Bad Company drummer Simon Kirke does likewise at Fulham Register Office. Jimmy Page, Robert Plant and John Paul Jones attend their reception in a Fulham pub.

16

Robert Plant joins Swansong recording star Dave Edmunds on stage at Birmingham Odeon.

October 1978

3

John Paul Jones and John Bonham participate in a "super-session" at Abbey Road studios, organised by Paul McCartney. Others present include Pete Townshend, Dave Gilmour and Hank Marvin. The results, two tracks titled 'Rockestra Theme' and 'So Glad To See You Here', will appear on the Wings album 'Back To The Egg'.

November 1978

The members of Led Zeppelin were based in London for six weeks of rehearsals, prior to recording their ninth album. Tax laws meant that the album, like 'Presence', would have to be recorded outside the UK, so the group could not afford the leisurely, piecemeal approach to album making that they had enjoyed in earlier years.

While in town, the group started being seen out and about a little more, after over a year of near invisibility. On November 1st, John Paul Jones and Robert Plant attended a raffle at the Golden Lion pub in Fulham, held in aid of a children's charity. And later in the month Plant appeared at a 5-a-side football tournament at Wembley.

December 1978

For three weeks, Led Zeppelin were in Stockholm at Abba's Polar Studios, working on the new album.

Robert Plant: **Abba were very kind and said why don't you come over and have a look at the** studios, because they reckoned it was really hot and it's sort of a weird place to go, Sweden. I mean, if you've got any choice at all, I think you might choose other alternatives. Like LA's got a pretty conducive mood for making raunchy records, although everybody seems to come out of there halfway on their knees by the end of the studio time. But to trek it to Sweden, in the middle of winter, a studio has to be so good – and it was, it was sensational and had just the right amount of live sound that we like.

Normally a regimental attitude has to be taken in the studio, but with Abba's studio it was very easy-going and the whole series of rooms beckoned for you to play good stuff and dictated the mood . . . along with the Swedish chemical beer.

They've got special homes for the people who drink it out there because they go loony after about three weeks, and that's how long it took us to make the album.

Jimmy Page: **It was a case of wanting to try a new approach to a lot of things. The environment was new, and one was practically a prisoner in the studio. It was more of a working project than a recreation ground. We went there with a project in mind – I'm not saying we had a 'job' to do – but we knew what we were doing and felt ready, having had some pretty good weeks of playing.**

During the Christmas period, Page continued working on the tapes at his home studio at Plumpton.

1979

January 1979

21
Robert Plant's wife Maureen gives birth to a son, Logan Romero.

February 1979

Jimmy Page, John Bonham and Robert Plant returned to Stockholm to complete the mixing of the new album.

Across the Atlantic, although not one single note of Led Zeppelin music had appeared on stage or on record for over a year, readers of 'Circus' magazine had voted Led Zeppelin as the World's Best Group, Jimmy Page as Best Guitarist, and Page and Plant as Best Song writers.

May 1979

Under the banner headline 'ZEP PLAY GIG SHOCK', the music papers announced that Zeppelin would be making their first live appearance in the UK since May 1975, and their first anywhere since July 1977, at Knebworth Festival in August.

The Festival was the latest in a series of mammoth events organised at Knebworth Park, near Stevenage in Hertfordshire, by promoter Frederick Bannister.

At the same time, it was announced that the gig would be Zeppelin's only live date during 1979 and that the new album would be released to coincide with it.

On a less grandiose scale, Robert Plant turned up at Stourbridge Wine Bar to jam with Melvin's Marauders (presumably somehow connected with Melvin Giganticus, see July 1978).

Jimmy Page, who had always shown a keen interest in the life of the community near his Scottish home, was in Caithness to unveil a plaque commemorating the rebuilding of the harbour by the inhabitants of the fishing village.

Jimmy Page: I just got up and said 'I'm not here for any political reasons whatsoever, but just from my own endeavours as an untrained musician. And it's just sheer determination that's been employed here against a good 80 per cent of the council who wished them to have no encouragement whatsoever.

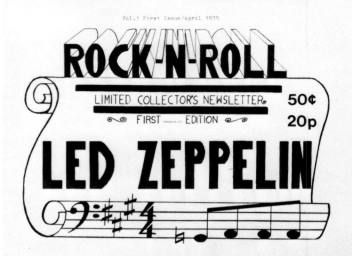

Portrait Photograph By Chris

Page 1

PHILLIPS HARBOUR
RE OPEN 1979
BY JIMMY PAGE
LED ZEPPLIN

June 1979

3
Tickets go on sale for Knebworth, although the support bill has yet to be finalised.

9
Robert Plant is interviewed on BBC's 'Saturday Rock Show' and looks forward to the Festival.

Robert Plant: It's the eternal problem of what to do first and what to do when, and we decided that we were in the mood to start playing again. There'll be new bits, bits from the past, maybe just a little bit different. I mean the thing is, if we have a rehearsal that lasts four hours and we run through all sorts of stuff, you can't interpret the same things that you were doing eight years ago identically. Things always change with Zeppelin, that's why after two years we can still get together and play and it makes

August 1979

4

The first Knebworth date, with Zeppelin supported by Fairport Convention, Commander Cody, Chas and Dave, Southside Johnny & The Asbury Jukes and Todd Rundgren's Utopia.

For the performance, Showco had brought across from the States the biggest system they had ever assembled . . . 100,000 watts of sound and 600,000 watts of light, including lasers. As at Earls Court, a huge video screen on the stage allowed everyone to see the group close up.

Zeppelin played for well over three hours, running through the same basic set as in Copenhagen, but with four encores – 'Stairway', 'Rock and Roll', 'Whole Lotta Love' and 'Heartbreaker'. The crowd loved it, even if the critics didn't.

11

The second Knebworth date, with Chas and Dave, Commander Cody, Southside Johnny, Utopia and Keith Richard's New Barbarians supporting. The set discards 'Ten Years Gone' in favour of 'Communication Breakdown', and press reaction was

sense. Rehearsals have gone really well and the new stuff is fitting in with the – ah – 'dinosaur' period. It's good!

26

All four members of Zeppelin attend a gig by Dave Edmunds and Rockpile, and go on to a reception afterwards.

28

John Paul Jones and Robert Plant go to a luncheon in aid of handicapped children, held at London's International Hotel. Jones pays £800 for a pair of tickets to the Wimbledon Men's Singles Final, which are offered in a charity auction.

The first Knebworth show (some 150,000 tickets) had sold out, and interest was so strong, not only in the UK but around the world, that a second date was added on the Saturday after the first one. This also had nearly sold out by the day of the Festival.

July 1979

24, 25

Copenhagen, Falkonerteatret.

As a warm-up for the Knebworth events, Zeppelin returned to the city where they had made their first appearance back in 1968, to play two low-key dates in a 2,200 seat theatre.

The first night was, by all accounts, pretty terrible but the second was much improved. The group's set included two new songs, 'In The Evening' and 'Hot Dog', and songs from every album except the first.

In addition to the try-out in Denmark, the group had also gone to Bray Film Studios, near Maidenhead, to experiment with some new lighting effects for Knebworth.

generally better than for the previous week.

Although the Knebworth dates had gone very well in most respects, it seemed there was little chance that they would lead to more intensive activity on Zeppelin's part.

Jimmy Page: **I think that the time has come for us to be working at a sensible pace, not massive slogs across the States. I'm not saying that there won't be any more long tours, but to do isolated concerts seems to be a wiser way of working. At the moment, everyone seems to be in that frame of mind.**

The first step is to do these gigs. If they come off it could be a workable situation doing just two or three gigs at a time. It gets a bit heavy doing very big sets, three days on and one day off. You come off these tours not knowing where you are, and have to go through a rehabilitation period before going out again.

20

The new Led Zeppelin album, 'In Through The Out Door', is released simultaneously around the world.

Reviews for the album were the most positive since 'Physical Graffiti', praising the production aspects of the record and

Zeppelin's capacity to keep developing with each successive release.

In the UK, where the New Wave phenomenon had all but taken over during the group's lengthy absence from the public gaze, 'In Through The Out Door' did hit the Number One spot, but was out of the Top Twenty before the end of October.

In the USA, however, it was at Number One for a record seven weeks and stayed on the Top Twenty until the end of February 1980. The album eventually sold over 4 million copies in America alone, reactivating all the other Zeppelin albums in the process, so that in late October they had all nine in the Billboard Top 200 at once.

November 1979

25
Robert Plant plays in a 5-a-side football tournament at Wembley (again).

28
John Bonham, John Paul Jones and Robert Plant attend the Melody Maker Awards ceremony at London's Waldorf Hotel to collect yet another amazing list of titles: Best Live Act, Band, Album, Guitarist, Producer, Composer and Male Singer.

December 1979

29
John Bonham, John Paul Jones and Robert Plant join the UNICEF 'Rock For Kampuchea' benefit concert at Hammersmith Odeon. Plant joins Dave Edmunds and Rockpile for a version of 'Little

Sister', and all three are part of Rockestra, an ad hoc group assembled by Paul McCartney with many of the musicians who had participated in his "supersession" of October 1978.

1980

January 1980

12
'Record Mirror' readers vote Knebworth the best gig of 1979.

16
K-Tel release 'The Summit', an album featuring performances from 13 top rock acts, the royalties from which will be going to The Year Of The Child. Led Zeppelin donate 'Candy Store Rock', from 'Presence'.

Robert Plant: Our friend from The International Year Of The Child asked me if I could think of any way at all that rock 'n' rollers or anything to do with the modern music business could contribute to The International Year Of The Child. So we drafted a letter and sent it to various bands and individuals that we thought would be good on a compilation album.

February 1980

Two more Readers Polls showed quite conclusively that, in America at least, Led Zeppelin were still beyond doubt the world's biggest rock band. 'Circus' readers voted them Best Group, Album, Guitarist, Male Singer, Songwriters, Producer and Drummer, as well as Comeback of the Year. The readers of 'Creem' went even further, putting the group and its members and product at the top of no fewer than 15 categories.

In sharp contrast, 'Sounds' back in the UK voted only Robert Plant as Best Male Singer and Knebworth as Best Live Gig.

April 1980

The members of Led Zeppelin got together in earnest for the first time since Knebworth to do a week's rehearsing at the Rainbow Theatre in London's Finsbury Park.

May 1980

Newspaper reports of Zeppelin's rehearsals leaked out, and soon they were forced to move to the New Victoria Theatre. Then, on May 17th, the purpose behind the sessions was revealed. The group would be undertaking a three-week, 14-date tour of Europe, as from the middle of June.

Away from all this activity, Jimmy Page was making another of his occasional forays on to the house market. For a rumoured £900,000 he picked up a little pied à terre by the Thames at Windsor, which had previously been owned by actor Michael Caine.

June 1980

For their first full-scale European tour since Spring 1973, Zeppelin scaled down their show slightly, playing an average of about 2½ hours of songs from every stage of their career, including three from the last album, and a resurrection of 'Train Kept A'Rollin" to open proceedings. Because the halls were relatively small by Zeppelin standards (4–10,000 capacity) there were also fewer special effects than on most of the group's tours in recent years.

17
Dortmund, Wastfalenhalle.

18
Cologne, Sportshalle.

20
Brussels, Forêt National.

21
Rotterdam, Ahoy.

23
Bremen, Stadthalle.

24
Hannover, Messehalle.

26
Vienna, Stadthalle.

27
Nuremberg, Messezentrum Halle.

This performance has to be stopped after three numbers because John Bonham is ill. It is diagnosed as physical exhaustion, and the drummer is less than fully fit for the rest of the tour.

29
Zurich, Hallenstadion.

July 1980

2, 3
Mannheim. Eisstadium.

5
Munich, Olympiahalle.

7
Berlin, Eissporthalle.

John Bonham: **Over all, everyone has been dead chuffed with the way this tour's gone. There were so many things that could have gone wrong. It was a bit of a gamble this one, but it's worked really well.**

Presumably this fairly relaxed, summertime jaunt round the Continent had been intended as a gentle return to the routine of touring after a three year lay-off. And it would appear that it worked extremely well as such. The concerts were ecstatically received and the musicians seemed genuinely pleased to be back in action.

September 1980

The group returned to England from their summer holidays to begin rehearsals for a month-long tour of the Eastern United States and Canada, set to open in Montreal on October 17th. They gathered at Jimmy Page's Windsor residence to start work.

25

John Bonham is found dead in bed at Page's house by road manager Louis LeFevre. The cause of death is not known at first, although the drummer had been drinking very heavily before and during rehearsals the previous day, and needed to be put to bed by Jimmy Page's personal assistant, Rick Hobbs. The police are called to the house, but there are no suspicious circumstances, and a post mortem is arranged to determine how Bonham died.

Tributes to Bonham poured in from all over the world, especially from fellow percussionists, as Led Zeppelin's future was once again thrown into doubt. The American tour was cancelled, but over the next few weeks, just about every able-bodied man who had ever twirled a drumstick was mentioned by some publication as a possible replacement.

October 1980

8

The inquest on John Bonham's death, at East Berkshire coroner's court, hears that he died (like Jimi Hendrix) from inhaling his own vomit, after a boozing session that took him through something like 40 measures of vodka in 12 hours. A verdict of accidental death is recorded.

10

The funeral takes place at Rushock parish church in Worcestershire, near Bonham's farm. It is a quiet, private service. Later, over 250 mourners, including many friends from the music world, attend the cremation ceremony.

December 1980

4

Swansong release a statement which announces: "The loss of our dear friend, and the deep sense of harmony felt by ourselves and our manager, have led us to decide that we could not continue as we were".

Postscript

The group's announcement did not put an end to speculation, and throughout 1981 various names were mentioned in connection with the vacant drum stool. There was even a rumour that the remaining members of Led Zeppelin were going to amalgamate with the remnants of Yes.

Meanwhile, they popped up from time to time in different places. Jimmy Page joined ex-cohort Jeff Beck during an encore at Hammersmith Odeon on March 10th, and spent much of the year working on the soundtrack for Michael Winner's film 'Death Wish II'. Robert Plant joined bands, both famous and unknown, on

stage (as had always been his wont), and on July 18th he appeared on BBC's 'Pop Quiz' sporting a fairly preposterous, shorter hairdo.

Then, at the end of the year, in

The birth of Led Yes?

RUMOURS of a 'supergroup' involving members of Led Zeppelin and Yes are gathering pace in rock business circles, although firm details are few and far between.

Essentially, it appears that Yes have now broken down following management hassles and the departure of Trevor Horn. Attempts are now being made to form a band with Yes and Led Zeppelin, who have been inactive since John Bonham's death last year, and there are reports that Geffen Records, who signed John Lennon and Yoko Ono as their first act last year, are bidding for the new band. Certainly they would be one of the very few companies that could afford the kind of advance that such a band could command.

What complicates these simple rumours is that various other 'big names' keep cropping up such as Rick Wakeman and Carl Palmer. This has led to further speculation that there may be not one but two 'supergroups' trying to get off the ground. Furthermore, promoter Harvey Goldsmith is reported to be ready to manage the band, but as he is in partnership with Brian Lane, former manager of Yes, each new twist to the story only raises more problems than it solves. Watch this space for further developments.

an interview with 'International Musician', Jimmy Page put an end to the possibility of Zeppelin continuing, once and for all:

Obviously, I really want to get out and play. I'd like to get a vehicle, a group of guys who will provide a vehicle for that, and that's the new project, sometime in the New Year.

It'll need some time to get together, because I don't want to do anything that isn't one hundred per cent terrific. It would be silly to even think about going on with Zeppelin. It would have been a total insult to John. I couldn't have played the numbers and looked round and seen someone else on the drums. It wouldn't have been an honest thing to do. No, it'll be new ideas, new material, and I'm dying to do it.

Albums

Led Zeppelin
Atlantic Records K 40031
Cas. K 440031

Good Times Bad Times / Babe I'm Gonna Leave You / You Shook Me / Dazed And Confused / Your Time Is Gonna Come / Black Mountain Side / Communication Breakdown / I Can't Quit You Baby / How Many More Times

Led Zeppelin II
Atlantic Records K 40037
Cas K 440037

Whole Lotta Love / What Is And What Should Never Be / The Lemon Song / Thank You / Heartbreaker / Living Loving Maid (She's Just A Woman) / Ramble On / Moby Dick / Bring It On Home

Led Zeppelin III
Atlantic Records K 50002
Cas. K 450002

Immigrant Song / Friends / Celebration Day / Since I've Been Loving You / Out On The Tiles / Gallows Pole / Tangerine / That's The Way / Bron-Y-Aur Stomp / Hats Off To (Roy) Harper

4 Symbols
Atlantic Records K 50008
Cas. K 450008

Black Dog / Rock And Roll / The Battle Of Evermore / Stairway to Heaven / Misty Mountain Hop / Four Sticks / Going To California / When The Levee Breaks

Houses Of The Holy
Atlantic Records K 50014
Cas. K 450014

The Song Remains The Same / The Rain Song / Over The Hills And Far Away / The Crunge / Dancing Days / D'yer Mak'er / No Quarter / The Ocean

Physical Graffiti
Swan Song Records SSK 89400
Cas. SK4 89400

Custard Pie / The Rover / In My Time Of Dying / Houses Of The Holy / Trampled Under Foot / Kashmir

The Song Remains The Same
Swan Song Records SSK 89402
Cas. SK4 89402

Rock And Roll / Celebration Day / The Song Remains The Same / Rain Song / Dazed And Confused / No Quarter / Stairway To Heaven / Moby Dick / Whole Lotta Love

Presence
Swan Song Records SSK 59402
Cas. SK4 59402

Achilles Last Stand / For Your Life / Royal Orleans / Nobodys Fault But Mine / Candy Store Rock / Hots On For Nowhere / Tea For One

In Through The Out Door
Swan Song Records SSK 59410
Cas. SK4 59410

In The Evening / South Bound Saurez / Fool In The Rain / Hot Dog / Carouselambra / All My Love / I'm Gonna Crawl